FLOWERS IN GLORY

Church flowers for
all seasons

by

Ann Prince-Smith

Tharston Press,
1989

I

Published in England by
Tharston Press
Morton Hall
Morton-on-the-Hill
Norwich
Norfolk   NR9 5JS

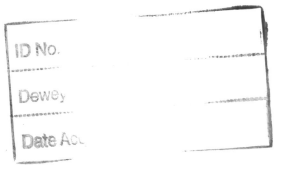

© Ann Prince-Smith, 1989
© Tharston Press, 1989

British Library Cataloguing in Publication Data:

Prince-Smith, Ann
    Flowers in Glory: Church Flowers for all Seasons
    1. Cathedrals.   Flower Arrangement
    I. Title
    745.92'6

ISBN 0-946696-07-1

Edited by Anthony Carter

Photography by Robert Ellis of Farrows using Hasselblad
equipment lit by portable studio flash heads.

Jacket designed by Simon Porter of
Farrows Graphic Design,
St Mary's Works,
Duke Street,
Norwich NR3 3AF

Typeset and printed by W. S. Cowell Ltd.
Ipswich, Suffolk, England.

Contents

Dedication	4
Acknowledgements	4
Foreword	5
Introduction	7
1. The Early Beginnings and Work of the Norwich Flower Guild	11
2. Easter Lilies	17
3. Maytime Blossoms	25
4. Summer Flowers and Special Events	31
5. Wedding Day	41
6. A Time of Thanksgiving	57
7. The Advent Ring	69
8. Christmas Celebrations	75
9. Winter Decorations	91
10. Myths and Legends	99
11. A Selection of Foliage for all Seasons	105
12. Flowers for all Seasons, in all Colours	112
Appendix I Finance and Ordering	118
Appendix II Tools of the Trade	120
Appendix III Glossary	123
Bibliography	125

Dedication

Dedicated to the memory of Elizabeth Powlett, Queen Bee of the Norwich Cathedral Flower Guild from 1972 to 1977, in gratitude for her inspiration and wise counsel.

Acknowledgements

I would like to thank all those who have been involved in the compilation of this record of our year's work. Many people, too numerous to single out by name, have helped in its preparation and I'm very grateful to them all. I must thank the Dean and Chapter of Norwich Cathedral for their continuous support, the Sacrist and Vergers for always being so helpful, the committee and members of the Flower Guild who so enthusiastically carried out the decorations included in this volume, and Mrs Mary D. Graves for kindly agreeing to write the foreword.

Mrs Marianne Brown, Dr K.G.Lindqvist, Mr Richard Hobbs of the Norfolk Naturalists Trust and Mr John Ayling of Hillier Nurseries (Winchester) Ltd all assisted in correctly identifying and naming the plants included in the text. Mrs Margaret Cobleigh helped by checking the American plant names and both Mrs Shirley Illingworth and Miss Lucy Paton helped prepare the glossary.

Anthony Carter edited the text, and this project would not have been possible without his help and advice. My daughter Lilla's encouragement and advice have also been invaluable.

I'm also grateful to Robert Ellis, the photographer, for his skill and patience throughout the year, Miss Jacqueline Reader for the photograph of Ben in his trailor, and Flora Dessica for donating the dried flower arrangement shown in Chapter 9.

Finally I must thank Miss Ann Todd for agreeing to draw the illustrations which so enhance the book.

The publisher will be paying the royalties from this book to the Friends of Norwich Cathedral.

Foreword

Those who know our lovely Norwich Cathedral will appreciate the beautiful flowers that are to be seen in various parts of the Cathedral throughout the Christian calendar, but to many visitors who come it must be apparent that love and care have been devoted to the array of flowers that abound therein.

I have been involved in many ways with flowers all my life, and never have I entered our Cathedral without being impressed by the beauty and size of the designs, particularly as flower arranging in a vast Cathedral is very different from arranging flowers in our homes or indeed our local Churches. The size of the building dictates the scale, but the problem is how to devise ways and means of creating such large displays, always with the thought of cost in mind, the plant material available at different seasons of the year, and also the difficulty of watering which is so important to keep the flowers fresh.

This tremendous task has been undertaken for many years by Lady Prince-Smith, who not only arranges some of the flowers herself, but who also organises a dedicated band of helpers, and in writing this book gives an insight into how it is all achieved, with the measurements, and the mechanics that she has devised, so that many people will be able to follow these instructions and create similar arrangements themselves.

Flower arranging should always be an enjoyment, giving pleasure to those who view and to those who create, and in this book both are very evident. I am sure that the delightful sketches will appeal to many readers.

For me personally it is a great compliment to write this foreword, and to have the opportunity of thanking Lady Prince-Smith and all her helpers for the lovely flower arrangements which are a continual reminder of the beauty of God.

Mary D. Graves
Past Chairman and President of NAFAS

A Floral Greeting at the South Door; An arrangement of chrysanthemums and lilies suitable for the thanksgiving service.

6

·INTRODUCTION·

his is not yet another book about church flower arranging; it has been compiled especially for the novice who has been asked to help in decorating a large church, cathedral or marquee for the first time, whether for a special occasion or for the weekly flower arranging roster. The large scale decorations described have to be prepared not only to celebrate the Church festivals, but for weddings and remembrance days.

As a member of the Norwich Cathedral Flower Guild for a number of years, I have found that the same questions and problems have recurred again and again. This book is an attempt to answer those queries, to guide the beginner through some of the main stumbling blocks, and to show how a large arrangement can be achieved without too much trouble. It is essential to realise that it really is very different to preparing the odd pedestal in a parish church. Many readers will be experienced and highly skilled members of flower clubs, but I hope there is also something for them in the ensuing pages which will assist them when it is their club's turn to prepare the flowers in their local cathedral or similar place of worship.

Why do we decorate churches, houses and other buildings with flowers? I have included some of the myths, legends and symbolism from which our present customs have evolved in Chapter 10. However, we have now progressed from the realms of legend to the reality of flower decorating to-day. The Dutch style, depicted in so many 17th century still life paintings, bears some similarity to modern design, although the mixture of fruit and flowers would not have been very successful as ethylene gas is produced from the combination.

Gertrude Jekyll's influential book *Flower Decoration in the House* was published in 1907. It brought about a great change in attitudes, and was a revelation to Edwardian women. Her writing encouraged a break from the hitherto accepted custom that the gardener alone should be in charge of decorating, usually on traditional lines. The author had firm views on how things should be done, but perhaps her most self-explanatory quotation arose from her remarks about table decorations, and I feel that it is equally applicable to any other facet of her beliefs one might choose:

> As in so many matters that concern social life, the treatment of the dinner table has always been subject to moods and vagaries of fashion. For a year or two one way of doing the table is 'the thing' when something else comes in; what was right two years ago is hopelessly out of fashion and some new crank reigns . . . With all these past and passing fashions, AS FASHIONS, I have nothing whatever to do. Good decorations in good hands have been done with all of them; and with every one of them good things may be done to this day if done just rightly. But surely it is best to keep the mind quite free, and to do the best one can with what one has at hand, whether the particular form of decoration happens to be in fashion or not.

Summed up simply, she told her readers to do whatever they liked. I heard a sermon recently which included the remark that 'We can be sure of the present and the future, but the past is uncertain.' I think this explains fashion very well, because it is our opinions that change continually, not the facts.

Fashions do change and individual taste varies considerably. Two people may hold very different views about the shape, colour and size of a planned arrangement, and may even differ over the choice of bowl. Everyone has personal likes and dislikes, so the equations are endless. In 1883 William Robinson wrote his book *The English Flower Garden* in which he discussed a less formal garden design, and encouraged people to break away from the rigid set patterns to try a fresher simpler approach, which applied equally to the flowers in the house. Elaborate Victorian and Edwardian decorations were frequently the work of professionals, either gardeners employed by the large houses or florists, and only comparatively recently have all sorts of people been encouraged to take an interest in flower arranging in creating different decorations. Between the two great wars Constance Spry created a minor revolution, or did she? I feel that she has been frequently misquoted, because she only continued the already established trend in persuading people to attempt something different, and encouraged a break from the formal stylised arrangements.

She also tried to persuade ladies to pick their own flowers rather than relinquishing the task to their staff. In the 1930s gardeners could not be expected to follow the current trend in decorating or to anticipate what would be needed, and often resented this interference in their domain. It was essential to make an ally of the gardener, not an enemy, for in 1937 Constance Spry wrote in the foreword to her *Flowers in House and Garden*, 'I am hoping that I may have furnished a little moral support to those of my friends who suffer from an autocrat in the garden, either the kind who makes flower-gathering feel like gun-running, or who destroys enthusiastic suggestions with irrefutable technical objections.' After fifty years and another world war, such autocrats are few and far between, but it was against this background that any change in ideas made slow progress. It

Left: This shed has served the Flower Guild since Mrs Paton donated it in the late 1940s. The Guild's work has now outstripped it, and we will be grateful to move into the new extension to the cathedral in 1989.

Right: Inside the Shed; Hardly a picture of order, more like chaos and inevitably whatever is required is either at the back or beneath a collection of wire netting and other items.

---

now seems hard to imagine that this sort of atmosphere existed even at the time when it was written.

Constance Spry encouraged people to 'consider a flower decoration as a piece of creative work to be designed and planned for a special purpose. Give what you can of time and material to create one good group rather than several indifferent arrangements.' The theme is repeated several times throughout this book, and for this I apologise in advance, but I hope when you have reached the last page, you will agree how important it is to put this theory into practice, especially in large buildings.

The Nave at Christmas

1

The Early Beginnings and Work of The Norwich Flower Guild

uring the late 1940s, before NAFAS was formed, Bishop H. St. Barbe Holland who had been appointed the Dean of Norwich Cathedral after returning from New Zealand, wrote to several people to ask them to help with the flowers in the cathedral. There had been none during the war years, so his request really started the Guild. He asked Mrs Joan Paton to organise the flowers; she lived in the Close and was therefore able to visit the cathedral daily to look after them. She bought the copper urns which we still use as well as the wrought iron stands and wall brackets. Although she began on her own, others were recruited to assist her, and until she moved from the Close, she dealt with everything. A small committee of three was formed to take over from Mrs Paton, but eventually it was decided that it would be better to have a co-ordinator and a few principal helpers. A new committee was formed to support the 'Queen Bee' and to help with the monthly organisation on a daily basis. Each committee member has a month on duty, supported by a number of volunteers, when she is responsible for making sure the flowers are well cared for and fresh. Her other duties include removing the dead or dying material, checking the watering, and reminding Guild members who have volunteered when it is their turn to do the flowers. The Flower Guild has continued to grow, and is today a flourishing organisation supported by over one hundred members and several flower clubs. (Queen Bee should not be confused with its American useage, where it refers derogatively to women who rise to power, and then make it difficult for others to challenge their position.) I certainly consider it a privilege to have followed in the footsteps of some talented predecessors. The main change over the last few years has been the vast increase in the workload due mainly to more and more special events, including weddings and concerts, being held in the cathedral. It is therefore essential that we have an experienced team as the nucleus in order to take on so much decorating, and to keep up a high standard. There are many aspects of flower arranging which I will not be covering in these chapters, so please remember that our subject is solely concerned with large decorations, not those intended for dining room tables or similar positions.

Flowers can be used like paints to create an artistic picture, and colours can be similarly used experimentally. Colours which are normally mixed together, can look entirely different when used on their own. White flowers left with their leaves on will not look as white as ones with their foliage removed. A mixed vase of blooms really needs blue included, but when this colour is used on its own it does not show up well, and always looks disappointing however magnificent the flowers are. These are just two examples of many, but they illustrate an important aspect which always needs careful consideration in order to make the best of any available material.

The decorations in Norwich Cathedral are the responsibility of the Flower Guild throughout the year. The Guild has a small committee with one person, usually referred to as the 'Queen Bee', acting as the co-ordinator between the Dean, Sacrist and the members. She is also the general organiser of all the decorating undertaken, which involves seeing the members of different organisations to see whether they have special requirements for their services. She has to talk to brides and their mothers, help them plan their flowers, and generally deal with any event in the cathedral from major festivals to the smallest family occasions. There are weeks when several separate events have to be co-ordinated, and these may have conflicting colour schemes. When this happens there is normally one event which takes precedence over the others.

The committee is carefully chosen, and each member usually has a number of years experience, having become familiar with the work through a type of apprenticeship. The qualifications required are varied, and begin with learning to cope with the large arrangements without always having pre-conceived ideas. It is not always possible to know what materials there will be to hand before one starts, and of course it helps if you have access to plenty of greenery or flowers, preferably both. It is also essential to have the time and energy to do the work, and the ability to work as part of a team.

Perhaps the last point is the most important, since a happy team is essential to the smooth running and success of the whole Guild whose main aim is to arrange the *Flowers for God*, to decorate the Lord's house and, through the flowers, to give pleasure and often spiritual uplift both to the regular members of the congregation and the visitors from home and abroad. This aspect of the work is the most rewarding and the most worthwhile. Whilst preparing the decorations one comes into contact with many visitors who frequently ask questions about the problems in preparing such large arrangements; they then usually want to know where they can find a cup of tea! It is always encouraging to hear words of appreciation, and although it can be rather daunting to have an audience, the pleasure given to so many people is certainly an important reason for doing the flowers. They are often the first and last impressions the visitors have of the cathedral.

Each committee member naturally has her own style, but they are all capable of co-operating to produce an overall scheme for the major events and festivals. Their individual differences help to form an overall impact, which is neither too set nor formal, and ensures that there is great flexibility. Weddings and festivals will be covered in the following chapters, and I hope that the detailed explanations will show how the work is carried out.

Nearly all the cathedral arrangements have to be planned on a three dimensional basis, as usually they are seen from at least three sides. This rules out having a flat decoration even though it may look very well from the front. It is also necessary to give depth to the flowers as this helps to show them up. I feel this is best summed up by saying that we arrange flowers, but we do not do set flower arrangements. In fact it would be true to say that we are decorators, a term once used to describe the gardener in charge of the flowers at great houses. Decorating also describes the efforts which encompass a number of events from a 'Midsummer Madness' to the glories of the Christmas Midnight Mass.

Before proceeding further, I must mention the help that the Vergers give us; they assist emptying and filling the heavy vases and move the large stands, they pull up hanging baskets from the triforium at Christmas, and go aloft in their climbing harnesses to fix the Advent ring. Much of our work would be impossible without their generous help and co-operation.

Flower clubs are situated all over the country and have a large and enthusiastic membership. The National Association of Flower Arrangement Societies of Great Britain was formed in 1959 in London. Members of NAFAS have done impressive work at flower festivals in churches, cathedrals and abbeys, and have helped raise many thousands of pounds towards the upkeep of these buildings.

I will now try and deal with the most common problems in more detail, and hopefully explain how they can be overcome.

PREPARATION

Difficulty in obtaining the right proportions is the problem most often encountered, this really must be right as everything else depends on it. For a start the containers will probably be much larger than any previously encountered. At Norwich Cathedral we use several deep copper urns which fit into the iron stands at the High Altar or into brackets on the nave screen. These are solid, deep enough to hold ample water, and can take good size branches. Washing up bowls are also frequently employed on pedestals, since these have a lip for fixing wire netting over the top allowing it to be then wired to the stand. Plastic window boxes or much larger plastic tubs are used on some of the tombs since stability and watering are not problems with these containers.

Once you have found the place where the flowers are to be prepared and discovered what sort of container is available, do take time to look round and think about the following:

(a) From where will it be viewed?
(b) How far away will it be seen, and will it be large enough?
(c) Is there an altar cloth or any other colourful item to be considered in the overall scheme?
(d) Are there any special seasonal requirements?
(e) Most importantly, what is the background or is it to be free standing?

It is best to sit down for a while and visualise what it may look like, remembering that if there is a large congregation, it will have to be seen over many heads, and hats! A few moments reflection at this stage can work wonders, and you will probably be amazed what occurs to you. A place like the nave will require a display at least 5ft (1.5m) tall, perhaps more, if it is to be seen from the west end. Do please forget those 3ft (0.9m) triangles seen so often on church pedestals. Their use is without doubt the most common mistake encountered, and usually results in a number of beautiful flowers being packed far too tightly to show up their true glory from anywhere beyond a few feet – it is such a pity, and a great waste of effort.

When you have considered all the above points, and decided on the colour scheme, you will want to know how to estimate the amount of material needed. There is no simple formula, but the following should give you some guidance. I personally think in tens, as it makes ordering simpler, although odd numbers are usually easier to arrange. A large pedestal, for example, will need a variety both in stem length and size. Five or seven larger flowers will give the whole arrangement a greater lift than if all are the same size.

The type of foliage and backing material will be dictated by the colour and variety of the available blooms. Well prepared fresh materials are essential and I would recommend quantity rather than quality, because too few expensive flowers tend to look lost. At this point, assuming that you have acquired all you need to start, we will deal with the more simple mechanics needed to prepare a good stable base for the materials.

In order to make a firm foundation for the majority of flowers a mixture of oasis and chicken wire is all that is required; oasis on its own is not strong enough. It must be well soaked, and I have found by bitter experience that it usually takes much longer to take up water fully than the makers suggest. If this is not done, and the centre remains dry, it cuts the life of the blooms considerably. It is always most important to remember that the flowers are to last at least a week, so avoid using too many bricks stacked on top of each other because it will dry up when out of water, defying all the good work of the waterers. It also shortens the life of the oasis as once it has dried out it does not readily take up moisture again unless boiling water is poured over the bricks. Next, take the chicken wire, usually 1-1 ½in (3-4cm) mesh, which will accomodate most plants, and pull it over the oasis, attach it round the vase, then wire it down on to the stand itself. Finally, top up with water before you start any arranging because most of the containers will take gallons – not the odd pint. Having finished the wiring, you should now be ready to both begin and enjoy your contribution to the decorating. I will consider the choice of materials next.

First, bear the arrangement's height in mind when you consider what foliage to choose, for in the Spring branches just coming in to bud are enough to give a beautiful outline, and provide the required height and width. The different foliage can form most of the display with just a few flowers placed in the centre at times when these are either scarce or funds are limited. The arrangement can be enlarged by having branches hanging down the container, and of course, if a washing up bowl is used it has to be covered with some foliage or flowers. We usually refer to the under foliage as the petticoats, and a wide variety can be used, but do avoid too heavy an appearance. If the back of the arrangement is visible, foliage can be employed to make it look not only neat and tidy but as a cover for the wire and foam. Some oasis may be above the rim of the container, but it will work well providing part of it is in the water to constantly draw up moisture. However, be careful not to make the common mistake of pushing a stem right through the oasis. Also do not underestimate how much foliage you need; it's far better to have too much than too little, because it is much easier to overcome a shortage of flowers. The lengths of the branches can be up to five or six feet, but these may be very heavy, and a lot of foliage requires not only careful handling but careful conditioning. Most material is much better if cut the previous day, and then given a long deep soak overnight. I prefer to take in larger branches, and cut from them as and when needed, because it will not hurt them providing they have been well soaked after cutting. A dustbin makes an ideal container, and as long as they are placed in a cool area, it is all that is required in most cases. Flowers and foliage requiring special treatment will be dealt with separately in Chapter 11.

Transporting all the material can prove quite a problem, which has to be tackled, but hatchback or estate cars are ideal for the job since they make getting everything in and out so much easier than when using a saloon model, and obviously the less the material is handled the better. Buckets can be a nuisance in a car causing havoc by at worst falling over or spilling even a small amount of water. Most flowers will travel well in big flat boxes, but if you do intend to transport some in water (wild flowers will benefit) a board on short uprights with the correct diameter holes to take the standard flower buckets will ease the problem. Having obtained all the foliage, there are still the flowers to find. Fortunately at Norwich the majority usually come from private gardens, and it is only when there is a large event, requiring a specific colour scheme, that we have to augment our normal supplies by approaching florists. As we proceed through the year there will be many examples proving that expensive flowers are not always necessary.

Before moving on to the Easter Festival, it is advisable, if you can find out when the flowers are normally prepared, to see for yourself what the vases look like empty, if you will have to work off steps, where the water is situated, and anything else that may help you plan the display well in advance.

At the High Altar; One of a pair displaying the Arum lilies at their best against a background of mixed foliage and forsythia. The lovely longiflorum lilies give the finishing touch, and will last for several weeks with care.

2

Lilies at Easter

uring Lent, when all the flowers have been cleared out, there is time to take stock of the flower shed's contents, and to clean the vases and the pedestals. It is at this time of the year that the committee meets to go through the programme for the coming year, and to discuss anything else which needs doing. The invitations to the annual coffee morning are sent out to all the Guild members, and since these number about 150.it is no small task to keep all the addresses up to date. Now that the details are on a word processor it is much easier to keep up with the never ending alterations, and it is now possible to do a mailshot by the same method. It is even necessary to check the obituary columns as I know to my cost when I telephoned to enquire why one of our members had not signed up; to my horror her husband announced that she had died three years ago. It is at this annual get-together that the Dean kindly says a few words, and volunteers sign up the rosters. The waterers are part of the Guild, and are usually drawn from people who live nearby, but are not flower arrangers. They are an indespensible band, considerably extending the flowers' lives which can be a great saving, whose work so often goes unnoticed except when someone forgets!

At Norwich, Easter is one of the occasions during the year that the committee prepare the flowers. They meet on Saturday morning to start the new season, all fresh oasis, wire to be fixed up, and pedestals to be put in place. Each member arrives fully loaded with anything she may have been able to acquire, and since where they are going to work has usually been settled before hand, they are able to start as soon as they arrive. Easter always seems to be associated with lilies and for some reason arums which seem to have a mind of their own. Preparing a matching pair of vases with about nine in each is hardly an easy undertaking! Portugal laurel is better than the native variety because it is not so heavy looking, but dark enough for the lilies to show up against. If you have a generous grower who will let you have some of the arum's own foliage it will make all the difference. It is best to set out the foliage and the outline in both of the containers before you add the lilies. White daffodils will mix in well and give added depth to the arrangement. They are also a help in keeping costs down providing the season is right for them. Arums are better if they can go straight into water as the stems tend to crush and clog up with foam, preventing them taking up moisture.

If blossoms are cut early enough they can be forced and brought into flower at the right time, forsythia is an excellent example. Spring flowers tend to have a brief life and are also short in stem, so they are ideal for smaller chapels or in the centre of the larger arrangements. Chapels, similar in size to most parish churches, require much smaller vases. The only point which must be noted is that they are seen from very close to, so that some of the tricks for making flowers go a long way cannot be used. They tend to use more flowers for their size than the larger ones.

Of all the Easter flowers I think the forsythias are the most versatile since the long sprays of gorgeous bright flowers and the beautifully curved shape of the branches make them just as good in small arrangements as the larger ones. Variegated privet with its lovely bright green and yellow leaves is possibly the most versatile of the foliage, often lasting up to three weeks, and is not limited to the Spring.

Easter cannot be passed without mentioning the Paschal Candle, a challenge requiring skill, patience and precision. Nor can it be dismissed when finished, for keeping it refreshed in the following weeks requires the same amount of dedication. The base of the candlestick is also decorated. The candlesticks, large enough to take the big plastic tubs, double as pedestals during the rest of the year. This means that they are not put away and forgotten for the greater part of the year.

THE HIGH ALTAR FLOWERS

Height (flowers only):	74in (1.8m)
Width:	55in (1.4m)
Mechanics	Wrought iron stands 58in (1.47m) high.
	Copper urn. Diameter at base: 10in (25.5cm)
	Diameter at top: 15in (38cm)
Flowers	*Euphorbia robbiae,* Spurge, Miss Robb's bonnet
	Forsythia x intermedia, Golden bells (US)
	Lilium longiflorium, Easter lily
	Mahonia japonica, Japanese mahonia
	Zantedeschia aethiopica, Arum lily
Foliage	Arum lily leaves
	Buxus sempervirens, Common box
	Cupressus sempervirens, Cypress
	Ligustrum vulgari, Common privet

At the High Altar there are a pair of wrought iron stands which hold copper urns securely, making them excellent receptacles for larger decorations. We are also fortunate in obtaining our lilies direct from the grower when they are at their freshest, and he kindly lets us have a generous supply of leaves to enhance their natural beauty.

The arrangement was prepared with some oasis about half way up the urn combined with chicken wire stretched tightly over the top and tied down onto the stand. Only minimum use was made of the oasis because lilies, being soft stemmed, are best in water alone. The foliage background helped to show off the white arums at their best, and allowed them to stand out at a distance. The cathedral's stone pillars are not easy to work against as their colour and size detract from the flowers, but greenery formed a backcloth for the display. Hazel catkins and pussy willow were incorporated to spread out the flowers, and they did not detract from the arums which had to remain the focal point. White daffodils mix in well and make the arums go further, but it is wise to avoid making the lilies appear too heavy and stiff. Their leaves usually hang over the urn covering the wire netting. I do think that natural foliage makes all the difference – do try and find a supply if possible.

The lilies we use often have stems over 3ft (0.9m) long and being very fresh can last over three weeks, although the cathedral's heat causes the foliage to die first. As long as the flow of water is not impeded the buds will open fully and sometimes change their direction, usually into an upright position.

These *Zantedeschia aethiopica,* Arum lilies, are one of the Flower Guild's main expenses during the year, but it can be alleviated if the congregation are asked to give donations towards the cost of the blooms, often buying one in memory of a relative. Some people seem to like to purchase their own, but this is not to be encouraged because you should be able to obtain a discount for a large number, and it does help to know how much has to be spent in advance. The display illustrated was finished with a *Lilium longiflorium,* Easter lily, donated by a member of the congregation. If the lilies are kept going for as long as three weeks, the cost becomes quite reasonable, and one tip to preserve them is to use a sharp pair of scissors to trim around their edges when they begin to brown.

If Easter is later there will be a much wider choice of both foliage and blossoms to mix with the lilies. Young larch shoots are delicate and can be easily bent to form petticoats in order to cover the wires. Pussy willow and wild cherry both mix well, and help to open and lighten the decoration. These can all be obtained free by walking around woodland. You ought to be able to find a sympathetic woodland owner to help you, and assuming that you have permission to pick, there are a few points you should remember before entering the wood. First, always inform the owner when you are likely to be collecting the material, do close all gates behind you, and never let dogs run loose as they may disturb the wildlife. Most importantly, take care that you cut as closely as possible to the main stem and never hack at the trees or bushes. Most woodlands are grown commercially as crops, but since pruning can be of benefit do not be put off.

Finally, do be careful when you are parking your car if you suddenly see just what you are looking for by the roadside. Only recently I saw a car illegally sticking out into the road alongside a stretch of double white lines whilst its owner resolutely attacked the hazel in the hedgerow with her secateurs.

THE PASCHAL CANDLE

Height overall:	72in (1.83m)
Bottom section:	44in (1.12m)
Width at top:	55in (1.4m)
Width at bottom:	44in (1.12m)

Mechanics, top:	Ring mould, 12in (30.5cm) in diameter, filled with oasis
bottom:	Three 8in (20cm) diameter bowls filled with oasis. All raised off the floor on a wooden base.

Flowers	*Alstromeria ligtu* hybrids, Peruvian lily, Lily of the Incas
	Chrysanthemums, white daisy spray
	Carnations, white spray
	Daffodils, yellow
	Daffodils, white/orange
	Daffodils, yellow/orange
	Forsythia Golden-Bells (US)
	Freesia, white

Foliage	*Adiantum capillus-veneris,* Maidenhair fern, Venus-hair
	Cytisus scoparius, Common broom, Scotch broom (US)
	Ligustrum ovalifolium 'Aureum', Golden privet
	Salix caprea, Pussy willow, Florist's willow (US)
	Stephanandra incisa

The Paschal Candle is the centre of the Easter Eve Vigil and its lighting a most moving moment in the ceremony. The arrangement must therefore be designed in such a way that it does not interfere with the candle lighting. The decoration will be on view from all directions, and at close quarters, so extra care must be taken to ensure that the flowers are fresh and of good quality to last well. They will have to be checked frequently to make sure that anything dead or wilting is removed immediately, and the gaps carefully filled with similar material.

The whole arrangement should compliment the candle and as far as is feasible point upwards like the broom and willow in the illustration. This decoration can be prepared in several different ways; a simple ring of Spring flowers can be just as attractive as the more formal efforts. After about two weeks the base arrangements are usually removed completely leaving the top ring decorated until Whitsuntide. In order to keep the Spring flowers fresh for as long as possible, the decoration requires both copious watering and regular spraying.

The ring mould filled with oasis is ideal as there is sufficient space to contain

The Paschal Candle; The highlight of the Easter decorations which requires time and patience
to prepare plus continual care until Whitsuntide. The High Altar is shown as it appears on
Easter Saturday with a completed vase of Arum lilies on the north side.

some water – a smaller mould would be just as suitable for a smaller candle. There are some rings made with removeable candle holders in them, and pottery rings can also be bought. The latter are not as easy to arrange as they only allow for a few small mainly upright flowers, although where it is difficult to keep renewing the material they can be a useful alternative. It must be stressed that a Paschal Candle decoration is very time consuming if it is to keep looking fresh until after Whitsun, and nothing looks worse than one containing dead flowers.

THE JESUS CHAPEL

Height overall: 88.5in (2.25m)
Width overall: 55in (1.4m) across the top section.

Mechanics   Metal pedestal
Bowl, oasis covered with wire netting
Jam jars to hold the daffodils upright at the back of the bowl.
2lb (0.9k) jar tied to the pedestal's upright.
Flat dish on the floor with a small urn shaped vase at the back.

Flowers   Daffodils, mainly yellow with a few pale varieties.
Primroses.

Foliage   *Hedera*, Ivy
Ligustrum ovalifolium 'Aureum', Golden privet

The Jesus Chapel arrangement depicted the ascent from earth to heaven as part of the Easter theme. The primroses, representing the earth, were placed in small jars standing on a flat dish. Although picked, they gave the appearance of growing, but providing plans are made well in advance pot grown flowers could be used in suitable containers, and would probably last longer. Ivy trails down and around the upright from the bowl on the pedestal, and all the daffodils reach upwards in a glorious splash of colour. The variegated privet was a very good foil for the flowers as it split them up, and lightened the effect of the display. The privet's yellow was exactly the right shade to blend in with the daffodils. The bowl was filled with blooms and became the crowning glory of this excellent example of what can be achieved with simple in season garden flowers. These can usually be obtained free at Easter even when it is as early as it was in 1988. The illustrated flowers were prepared on the 2nd April and lasted a full week, which was a good result for so early in the Spring.

It does help if daffodils still in bud are used, although the aim should be to have

The Jesus Chapel; This simple arrangement of early Spring flowers shows up well in the chapel, and harmonizes with the splendid *Adoration of the Magi* by Martin Schwarz.

them looking their best on Easter Sunday. A mixture of buds and open blooms can be used to great advantage. Oasis is best kept to a minimum as daffodils are much better in water, and can last up to two weeks in a cool place. If oasis is used care must be taken not to damage the stems when they are pushed into it, as it can block them and thereby shorten their lives. It is important that an arrangement like this is checked frequently·to remove flowers at the first signs of wilting since it is surprising how quickly a good decoration can turn into a very sad sight. It is worth noting that the decoration blends well with Martin Schwarz's *Adoration of the Magi*, painted in 1480, and one of the cathedral's treasures.

A display of early Spring flowers with hollow stems will need large regular

Blossom at the West End; A mixture of early blossom with different foliage added to help give it shape and substance. The screen vases can be seen in the distance.

quantities of water until the day they die. No amount of preparation and long soaks before use will prevent their need for daily attention.

Decorating a small chapel, I have been fortunate in having pot-grown arum lilies flowering at Easter. These were placed at the foot of the candlestick, and remained fresh for weeks. To avoid any chance of their drying out, the pots were stood in saucers filled with water. Do not forget that these lilies in their natural habitat like to grow in streams, and should not have the flow of water up their stems interrupted. If this happens the stems become limp, and the flowers quickly fade.

3

Maytime for Blossoms

hese two copper urns normally hold the largest arrangements in the cathedral, but even at this size they can hardly be seen from the west end of the nave. The pink blossom looks lovely on its own but does not show up very well, however a backing of bright green beech leaves and some young shoots of *Malus* with the leaves just coming out will help enormously to show the blossom to the best of its true glory. There is only one way to deal with these branches which have a will of their own; place them in the urn in the way they demand to go. This will show up the flowers in the same way as when growing naturally, some blooms will hang down, some face left, and some to the right, just as they grow on the trees. In order to avoid waste it is best to sort out a few of each direction when you pick them, then before you start work on the vases, divide the acquisitions into two heaps again insuring that there are a few of every type for each vase. This planning will ensure that you do not travel miles with a car load only to find that most of them hang down!

If you are fortunate to have some easily available blossoms it will be a bonus, but if a kind friend offers some do take care how you prune the trees if you want to be asked back a second time. The same words of caution apply to magnolias since all large flowering shrubs and trees have to be cut very carefully. Magnolias can look-glorious – even a few large branches on their own in a vase are all that is required for an impressive display.

Beech leaves do not like being picked when too young. It is possible to force them early, but they last much better if left to come out on the tree. The same applies to the larch, and both make an excellent foil to the blossoms. It is impossible to plan too far in advance because each year is different, but do not be afraid to experiment and be prepared to use whatever is available at the time. *Sorbus Aria,* whitebeam, is another lovely foliage to mix with pink cherry blossom because the young light grey leaves compliment the blossom so well.

The two vases are often decorated by two members of the Flower Guild working together, or a flower club will undertake to do them one week with several members arriving for a joint effort. Either method works well because the vases have to be prepared working from short steps, and the task is made much easier if there is a helper to pass up the material or to stand back and give helpful advice on how it looks from a distance. It is just not possible to work on these vases without the use of steps unless the arranger is over six feet tall! The same problem arises over watering although I have known one lady balance a can on her head and gradually tip it. She had perfected the art over many years, but the risk of an unnecessary bath is such that it is not a method I would recommend.

The two illustrated arrangements were prepared by two ladies each preparing one of the vases. This method is successful if you are used to working together, but only comes after a lot of practice. It is particularly useful when tackling a large event with a number of big decorations requiring some symmetry. In these two, common beech was used as backing with *Prunus* 'Kanzan', a bright double pink cherry blossom, as the principal blooms, and therefore the dominant colour. Crab apple blossom was used to fill in and give the arrangement depth. The lovely trailing larch branches act as petticoats over the urns, helping to show up the drooping blossom. From the size you can see that many of the branches are over 6ft (1.8m) long and several of the beech have a spread of over 5ft (1.5m).

THE NAVE – TWO ALMOST MATCHING DECORATIONS

Height:	96in (2.44m)
Width:	100in (2.54m)
Mechanics	Iron brackets, 20in (51cm) high, fixed to the screen holding copper urns, 15in (38cm) in diameter. The height from the top of the urn to the floor is 72in (1.83m). A small amount of oasis and chicken wire is stretched over the top and fixed firmly to the bracket with wire.
Flowers	*Malus pumila*, Crab apple, light pink
	Malus, Crab apple, dark pink
	Prunus 'Kanzan', Cherry, double pink
Foliage	*Fagus sylvatica*, European beech (US)
	Larix decidua, European larch (US)

A large pair of two-handed pruners are essential to cut through the thicker stems since secateurs are not sufficiently strong. One committee member sensibly arrived with her own long handled pruners for a little work on the Cathedral Close trees. Two people are certainly needed to carry some of the material to where it is required in the cathedral, as simply negotiating the doors can be a problem for one person working alone. One of the best ways to cope with this task is to use a donkey cloth, a five foot sheet with handles at each corner, which allows two people to carry an enormous amount of stuff. It can be placed in the back of a car, the material piled onto it, and on arrival carefully pulled out without crushing the blooms or damaging the foliage. These donkeys are also excellent for taking all the dead or unwanted material to the rubbish tip.

The blossom and all Spring flowers require vaste quantities of water. I can not stress too much that they will need daily topping up to keep them fresh, and for this you must have waterers who live nearby. The first twenty-four hours are crucial, and if there is an extra large event the flowers will use far more water and a good spray will cheer them up. If the blooms are once allowed to droop they will not recover, and all the effort of cutting, gathering and arranging will be wasted. It is not surprising that volunteers to do the flowers at this season are hard to find.

Prunus avium, the wild cherry is very pretty and can be kept going for over two weeks. It does require a nice light position to show up to its best advantage, and if it is cut in bud its bright green shoots will come out in time, continually altering the decoration's appearance. It is not suitable for a set piece where change would be a disadvantage, but it can give a lot of pleasure for very little cost. There are a number of *Cytisus* varieties, ornamental brooms, which will blend with the white cherry blossom.

Petal drop is a problem with all blossoms since it needs clearing up regularly, and it is essential to remove the foliage before it dies completely, otherwise the mess is dreadful and worse than confetti inside the building.

THE WEST DOOR

Height:	70in (1.78m)
Width:	86in (2.19m)
	Viewed on a curve of approximately 240 degrees
Mechanics	Pedestal, 52in (1.32m) high
	Green washing up bowl, 12in (30.5cm) diameter, placed on the top.
	Oasis, a small quantity placed below the water line, chicken wire on top, tied down to the pedestal.
Flowers	*Malus pumila*, Crab apple
	Prunus 'Kanzan', Cherry, double pink
	Rhododendrons, pink and pale pink
Foliage	*Fagus sylvatica*, Common beech
	Helleborus occidentalis, Lenten rose

The arrangement at the great West Door is the first one seen by most visitors when they enter the cathedral. It forms a welcome to the many thousands who come every year, playing a special part in the life of the cathedral since first impressions so often have the greatest impact. The pedestal stands by a pillar at the south-west corner near the door, and it must be a good stable example if the crowds are not to knock it over as they brush past.

It can be seen from the illustration that the display is seen on a curve of about 240 degrees and therefore has no real front view. The contents are similar to those in the urns at the nave altar, but because it is seen at such close quarters more attention to detail has to be given. The hellebores and rhododendrons are ideal for infilling, the washing up bowl makes a stable container, and with the wire netting over the bowl attached to the pedestal every precaution is taken to prevent an accident happening. The stone pillar has a nail conveniently placed allowing some of the heavier foliage to be attached to it when necessary. A central branch helps act as a stabiliser for the whole display.

This arrangement uses a lot of material, and it is often prepared to compliment the screen vases as they can be seen together, although they are about 175ft (55m) apart. The distance from the flower shed and the unloading points makes the use of a low loading trolley, of the type used in garden centres as plant carriers, a great benefit which saves considerable energy. Everything including a pedestal, container and water can be loaded and taken the length of the nave in one trip, whereas before several journies had to be made. The tall pedestal for the Paschal Candle, normally reserved for special occasions, is also used for very large arrangements with a big plastic tub. Steps are needed to complete a display and firm ones with a good platform and a handrail are best. A lot of pushing and reaching is usually necessary to display the material in the right positions, and light aluminium steps do not have enough stability.

Whilst on the theme of Spring blossom mention must be made of apple and pear which looks beautiful on their own. You may know of someone who has an old orchard, but be careful not to vandalise good fruit trees. These blossoms can be forced for an early date providing they are picked in good time. I greatly regret having a pear tree chopped down after years of trying in vain to do something with the prolific crop which closely resembled bullets in shape and texture. If only I had given it a last glorious opportunity to give some pleasure to a wider audience. If anyone is considering planting flowering trees try and plan for a continuity of blossom. It is possible to have different varieties out over a period of several weeks with a wide choice of colour, most of which will blend together. A good nurseryman will advise a planting plan covering the whole range of flowering times and help choose the colours ranging from deep pink to white in doubles, semi-doubles and singles. The foliage will vary from soft apple green to deep copper. After the early crab and cherry trees progress continues with all types of lilacs followed by the enormous variety of azaleas and rhododendrons.

It is interesting to find that in 1913 William Robinson stated in his book *The English Flower Garden* in the chapter entitled 'The Flower Garden in the House':

This is important, in view of the many shrubs that flower in our climate in spring, and of which, if flowering shoots are cut when in bud, the flowers open slowly and well in the house. They are best placed in Japanese bronze or other opaque jars. The taller Japanese bronze jars with narrow necks are very useful for these, and it is excellent practice to cut the bud-laden shoots of Sloe, Plum, Apple, Crab, and like plants, and put them in jars to bloom in the house. By this means we advance their blooming time; and, in the case of severe weather, the beauty of early shrubs may be lost to us unless we adopt this plan. We see how well the French practice of growing Lilac in the dwelling-house prolongs the

At the Nave Screen; Two large vases containing cherry blossom from the Close suitably backed by branches of young delicate beech leaves.

---

beauty of this shrub, and it is not difficult to do something of the kind for the hardy shrubs and early trees that come with the Daffodils, but are not so well able to brave the climate. These shoots of early shrubs are also usually best arranged each by itself, though some go well together, and graceful leaves of evergreens may be used with them. One advantage of dealing with one flower at a time is that we show and do not conceal the variety of beauty we have. For, all thrown together, that variety will be much less evident than if we make clear the colour and form of each kind. Some proof of this may be seen in the work of the best flower-painters. In the work of M. Fantin-Latour, for example, his nosegays of many flowers, evidently bought at some market stand, are painted as well as his simple subjects, but these last are far the best pictures. However, there is such a wide range of plants, shrubs, and woodland and hedgerow flowers, that we must not hesitate to depart from any general idea if it tends to keep us from making the best of things in simple and ready ways.

LEAVES.– Many as are the flowers of the open air excellent for house, the leaves of the open air tree or shrub or plant are hardly of less use for the same end: notably the foliage of evergreen shrubs in warm and sea coast districts, from evergreen Magnolia, Poet's Laurel, Cypress, Juniper and Thuja, Cherry Laurel, and Bamboo; even in the coldest districts we have the evergreen Barberry, and more than fifty forms of the best evergreen climbers, the Ivy, and the Holly with its scarlet, yellow, or orange berries. The trees in autumn give us leaves rich in colour – Maple, Medlar, Mespilus, Parrottia, Tulip-tree, and many others. The shrubs and climbers, too, help – Bramble, Wild Roses, Water Elder (Viburnum), Common Barberry, with its graceful rain of red berries; Vines in many forms; hardy flowers, too, help with Acanthus, Alexandrian Laurel, Solomon's Seal, Iris, Plantain Lily.

It is nice to think that we are carrying on a well established tradition, and perhaps we can learn from William Robinson. Barberry is now known as *Berberis vulgaris* and Plantain lily or *Funkia sieboldi* as *Hosta sieboldiana*.

The early Spring and Summer months always provide a good selection of blossom and foliage for preparing large scale decorations in any sort of building at minimum cost. The many varieties of *Crataegus,* hawthorn, are most attractive, but some people believe they attract insects indoors so it is best to first check whether they are acceptable. Branches of young oak leaves can be used at this time of the year as their leaves are much brighter than most similar foliage. *Fagus sylvatica* 'Riversii' is one of the best copper beeches as it retains its lovely deep colour throughout the Summer. Young maple is also useful although it does tend to look heavy later in the season. Do try different foliage plants, and if you are not sure about them put some in a bucket at home to see if they take up water as not all greenery cuts well. If you trim the bark off the last two inches and split the stem, then give them a good soaking overnight, you will be able to see how they react when cut. The subject of greenery and its preparation is dealt with in more detail in Chapter 11.

4

Summer Flowers and Special Events

o sooner have the May blossoms and early Summer flowers passed, than Midsummer arrives with its wonderful choice of flowers from the herbaceous borders. The chrysanthemums, for so long a stand-by, can at last be set aside until later in the year.

One benefit gained from working with limited funds is that we are forced to look carefully at what is available, ensuring that there is constant change and variety in the decorations. Today, if cost is not a factor, it is possible to obtain the same flowers almost throughout the year, and this can lead to stereotyped arrangements. Some years ago I met a clergyman's wife, who had recently moved to a new parish where I knew there was an enthusiastic flower club, and when I asked about the church flowers, I was told: 'Oh, only the colour changes, one week pink, another yellow, and so on.' I later visited a flower festival held in their church, and she was certainly right because, with hardly an exception, the flowers were monotonous, rigid and unimaginative, and in my opinion hardly in keeping with the surroundings.

High Summer is often dominated by a programme of major events requiring extra large, and long lasting decorations. The weather usually dictates the choice of flowers, so unless a large order from a florist is anticipated, there is little benefit from planning too far ahead. If the flowers are being purchased in bulk, ten days to a fortnight in advance is usually a safe time to place an order, because it gives the florist or nurseryman time to check that the required blooms are available before he orders, but do allow extra time if there is a bank holiday. It will also give you time to change the order if a particular flower is either too expensive or unobtainable. Prices do fluctuate considerably and if you order commercially do not forget that Value Added Tax will be added to the total; it is especially important if you have a limit on your spending.

Providing the weather has been kind, there will be a wonderful choice of excellent garden flowers from the large blooms of delphiniums, peonies and phlox to the small dianthus.

The choice will of course vary over several weeks depending on the weather, and unfortunately a lot of the plants with delicate flowers are very easily damaged. Roses are perhaps the most delicate blooms we ever use, because the petals are so easily spoilt by rain and strong wind in a matter of minutes. If the flowers are needed the same day, it is always best to cut all material before the morning's heat reaches its height. Good roses are more likely to be found in bud early, as they open as the day progresses. After preparation they can be held back by leaving them in a very cool dark place in deep buckets of water (see Chapter 12). Gladioli can also be similarly treated, and their flowering delayed to suit the time when they must look their best. The gladioli corms can be planted in rotation to provide a supply over a long period, although I have to admit that whenever I have planted in advance for a special occasion, or opened my garden, I have never judged it correctly.

In this chapter I shall try to deal with the problems that occur when the cathedral and cloisters have to be decorated for a special event. Problems arise at every stage from the initial planning, through ordering to the day when the arrangements have to be prepared. I have chosen the first weekend in July 1988 to illustrate these points, because not only was there the annual gathering and general meeting of the Friends of Norwich Cathedral, but in the same week the British Medical Association held its adjourned AGM in the cathedral.

The Friends' meeting began with a service in the nave on Saturday morning, followed by luncheon in the cloisters, then the AGM in the nave during the afternoon. The flowers had to be positioned where they could be seen at their best by as many friends as possible, and where they would not interfere with the free movement of visitors to the cathedral.

The British Medical Association's 156th AGM was hosted by the Norwich branch, the first time since 1874 that it has been held in this city. The meeting started with an ecumenical service in the cathedral on Sunday evening, and on Wednesday evening the adjourned AGM was held in the nave followed by the Presidential Reception in the cloisters. The choice of flowers was influenced by the two events being held several days apart, because only blooms able to last at least a week could be considered.

This particular event was held in close liaison with the BMA, and we were fortunate that a member of the Flower Guild was appointed to look after their interests, and to be responsible for ordering the flowers which the association was kindly donating. The first telephone discussion took place many months in advance which enabled us to keep some of the roster places clear for the BMA ladies who wished to take part in the decorating.

A few weeks before the event a meeting was held in the cathedral to look round, and decide finally where the flower arrangements would be required. It also gave some of the helpers an opportunity to see what they would be expected to tackle, and to find out where everything was kept. A timetable was carefully worked out to plan for the arrival of the flowers and greenery, and finally, a rough list was compiled to act as a guide for ordering the florist's blooms. (See Appendix I, Finance and Ordering)

The BMA's requirements were that most of the arrangements should reflect the association's own red, blue and gold colours. In order to cut down the overall cost, it was decided that the cloisters should remain outside the planned colour scheme, and that they would be decorated with whatever was available on the day. Other Guild members, who were decorating the High and the Nave Altars, did their best to adhere to the colour scheme, and were most successful in doing so.

Arrangements were made for the flowers to be delivered on the Thursday in order to give them a thorough soak over night in a cool place. They were placed underneath the cathedral treasury, conveniently near the door leading to the flower shed and water taps. The greenery, for the most part, was kept in various containers outside. It is important to borrow enough of these for so large an event, and when we miscalculated a kind garden centre helped by supplying extra buckets.

Two members of the Guild committee went into the cathedral on the Thursday to prepare the extra containers, soak the oasis, and cut the wire netting to the required sizes. The pedestals and vases were then positioned, and filled with water to facilitate an early Friday morning start. When planning a big event, never underestimate the time that this preparatory work will take to carry out.

The largest arrangements were to be displayed in large green tubs, with the minimum amount of oasis, to give them the benefit of plenty of water, and would be high enough to be visible above the heads of several hundred delegates. These arrangements still looked fresh a week later, and were in the correct position to decorate the nave for an ordination service, the altar having been brought forward in line with the lectern and pulpit.

Blue is a notoriously difficult colour, but the clear shade required, without a trace of mauve, was adequately represented by using delphiniums, larkspurs, some scabious and *Aconitum napellus,* monkshood. Lilies and gladioli represented the gold in the BMA's colours, while pinks and more gladioli were used for the bright red, avoiding shades of scarlet. Spray carnations might have been better than the pinks, but the pinks were available although in this case they were the first to wilt. The small spray carnations are some of the most versatile flowers, and excellent value if they have to be purchased.

Foliage was chosen to blend with and enhance the colour scheme, and copper beech, maple and purple leaved plum proved particularly effective when combined with a fair amount of variegated foliage like privet, elaeagnus and hosta leaves.

Extra arrangements in the BMA's colours were prepared in the nave, the lectern, pulpit, west door, and on two of the tombs. An overall colour scheme certainly gives more impact to the general effect. In order to keep the cost within a set budget, the vases at the crossing of the transepts, the south door, and the chapels were done in white and peach to blend in with the overall scheme. One chapel looked very pretty with blue and white blooms. It does pay to plan a week ahead, because some of the pedestals were adapted for a wedding the following week. Nothing was wasted or thrown out prematurely.

It was most appropriate that the committee members included a relation of John Green Cross, founder of the BMA's Norfolk branch in 1835. In 1846 he was President of the 14th Annual Meeting of the Provisional Medical and Surgical Association, held in Norwich. He is buried in the cloisters, and flowers were placed on his grave for the reception. Other committee members working on the decorations included a nurse and a surgeon's daughter. The ladies representing the BMA completed four of the arrangements, while the rest, including those in the cloisters, were undertaken by the committee members and a few helpers. There were twenty-four different arrangements, of which five were in the cloisters, placed carefully to avoid interfering with the refreshments in such a large area.

This magnificent pedestal arrangement near the Nave Altar was the principal decoration for the BMA meeting, and clearly shows the problems we face in avoiding the many loudspeakers and the banners.

The west and north sides were chosen for decorating, and also the book shelves in the north-east corner by the Prior's door. The shelves are three alcoves in a row situated above the steps leading to the door, so to avoid uniformity the central alcove had an arrangement displayed in a small stone garden urn, and the outer ones placed in lower bowls. This dark corner is notoriously difficult to decorate, but one of our members has a house near the cathedral's east end, and she most conveniently had a number of beautiful alstromerias ready at the right time, which showed up well in spite of the light. These exquisite flowers, with a few pieces of white material and some light variegated foliage, brightened up the corner perfectly. The decorations on the north and west sides are dealt with later in this chapter.

The cloisters are the largest in Europe, and their massive size presents a problem, because they require enormous decorations to have any impact at all, and these large, bold arrangements have to withstand a certain amount of wind. Consequently, only the largest and most solid containers are suitable, and once, when a copper vase was used, it was blown off one of the stone columns on the north side. Pedestals of any kind lack stability and should only be used indoors. There was an occasion, several years ago, when a predecessor of mine decided to place a pedestal with a beautiful blue and yellow display at the entrance to a marquee which had been erected in the cloisters. The wind increased until it blew the whole arrangement over, not once but three times, before enough wires were attached to anchor it safely. This was acheived with the help of her husband who fortunately arrived at the crucial moment. Disaster was averted because the display had been so well prepared that when it fell not one bloom was dislodged, and the visiting VIP saw nothing amiss when she arrived.

There are two large glass tanks, 21 ½in (53cm) high, 12in (30cm) wide and 8in (20cm) deep, which we sometimes use in the cloisters. They are very heavy, hold an ample supply of water, and the flowers last well in them. When filled, their weight becomes a problem, and they are impossible to empty without asking for the Vergers' assistance. I have to stress again that it is essential to check the water level, and to make sure the display is sprayed regularly if the flowers and foliage are to last and look fresh for the full duration of the event. When the BMA held its meeting, we found it necessary to water and check the flowers every day. The large numbers of delegates present and the constant stream of tourists in July caused a high degree of transpiration, always a problem in hot weather or when the cathedral is heated during the winter. Transpiration is the process whereby the roots take up moisture which is then secreted through the leaves to cool the plant. The amount of moisture given off depends on the atmospheric humidity. If there is a check in the process, leaves fall off and the plants will wilt rapidly. Plant transpiration is analogous to perspiration in animals.

The black and white photograph shows a tall dramatic decoration near the lectern in the nave, and it is a good example to illustrate some of the many problems which have to be overcome. The loudspeakers are perhaps the most obvious since they are positioned throughout the cathedral, and as they have to be left uncovered, they too frequently give the impression of growing out of the arrangements, unfortunately more often than not at the top. Depending where the speakers are secured to the pillars, they can often give the decorations a lopsided appearance. The shiny ones, as illustrated, catch the eye immediately becoming the focal point, and detract from the flowers. Loudspeakers and water do not mix, so great care has to be taken when spraying. The banners are another hazard, because these too must be kept dry, and permanent damage can be caused by allowing some types of flowers to touch the material causing stains. It is essential that such problems are given due consideration.

The seating in the nave can be moved, and rearranged with considerable flexibility. When the illustrated pedestal was finished, the flower arranger found all the seating had been moved back, leaving an unexpected clear space in front of the display which altered the planned effect considerably. In this case the seating had been moved in order to bring the altar forward from the nave sanctuary, and when this happens consideration has to be given to the amount of movement in the area close to the pedestal. Robed clergy take up a lot of room, and can so easily catch the flowers with disastrous results. Some time ago an attractive pedestal arrangement toppled in the middle of a service, but was caught by an alert Verger, just before it went over. There is a raised platform which can be placed between the lectern and pulpit, and used as a concert stage. I have tried moving a pedestal into position after an orchestra has set up the music stands, and it is not easy. Larger pedestals set firmly on the ground are much preferable, and can stay in position after the stage has been removed.

Lighting has to be taken into account, as it never seems to be in the right place or pointed in the right direction, wherever the arrangements are placed. If it is possible, the light should fall on the flowers making a tremendous difference to the overall effect. Light shining from behind through the arrangement should be avoided at all costs, because the effect is to create a black blob, which is extenuated in the darker wintry days. At Christmas, when the days are so short, lighting can make or completely spoil the decorations. There are many points to consider when choosing the best place for a pedestal display, and only experience of the building combined with a knowledge of all the special requirements will solve all the problems raised. Twenty-four arrangements in an area as large as Norwich Cathedral and its cloisters may not seem many, but a few decorations of the correct proportions, and so well positioned that they can be seen to their best advantage, are much more effective that a larger number of small or badly placed vases. Whilst on my travels I visited another cathedral, and found a number of attractive pedestal arrangements in the nave, but the overall effect was totally spoilt by their uniformity, since all were the same height, and their flowers almost identical. In fact the rest of the flowers around the entire cathedral were of a similar mix and shape, with hardly an exception. No doubt a great deal of trouble and care had been taken to prepare the flowers, but if only someone had walked to the west end to imagine how the pedestals would look when the nave was full of people, they would immediately have seen the problem, and adjusted the heights of some of the stands accordingly. It is so disappointing to see beautiful flowers in an empty cathedral, and realise that hardly any of them will be seen or appreciated during a service or concert, except for the few people sitting close to one of the arrangements.

For Summer Celebrations; The cloisters' flowers were arranged in a bath tub on a shelf which runs the length of the west wall, and the display's size made it visible from a large area. To combat the problem of the elements the contents were chosen with great care and consideration, and the arrangement proved resilient to both wind and rain.

THE CLOISTERS – WEST SIDE

Height overall: 78in (1.98m)
Width overall: 75in (1.9m)

Mechanics   Bath tub, zinc, 27in (68.5cm) long, 18in (45cm) wide and
10½in (26.5cm) deep

Foliage	*Asparagus officinalis,* Asparagus, culinary
	x Cupressocyparis leylandii, Leyland cypress
	Elaeagnus pungens 'Maculata'
	Fagus sylvatica, Common beech
	Hedera, Ivy, flowering
	Prunus lusitanica, Portugual laurel
Flowers	*Alchemilla mollis,* Lady's mantle
	Alstroemeria ligtu hybrids, Peruvian lily
	Anthriscus cerefolium, Giant chervil
	Campanula persicifolia, Peach leaved bellflower
	Delphiniums, white hybrids
	Echinops ritro 'Veitch's Blue', Globe thistle
	Hemerocallis citrina 'Baronii', Day lily
	Lysimachia punctata, Yellow loosestrife
	Salvia sclarea 'Turkestanica', Sage
	Sambucus racemosa 'Plumosa Aurea', Golden elder

A bath tub is perfect for using in the cloisters, because it fits onto the stone ledge, is stable, and holds a large quantity of water. The greatest difficulty is to find a way of successfully securing the heavy branches in place. In the illustration a tall piece of common beech was stuck to the wall with some 'Stay Soft' flower base, as it had proved impossible to attach the tall branch to the small nail although it was in the right place. Some bricks were put in the bottom of the tub, and a mixture of oasis and chicken wire was used to support all the material needed to fill this container. If you undertake this sort of task, do make sure the oasis blocks are wedged securely to stop them moving around. Smaller containers can be incorporated into the foundations if required, and the wire then stretched over the top. In order to raise the level of the oasis at the front, upturned plastic containers (ice cream cartons) were placed beneath the blocks and wedged in position.

It is essential to have enough greenery to cover the tub's front, because it is hardly a thing of beauty. During the 1987 Flower Festival a large arrangement was prepared in a bath tub, further to the south on the west side of the cloisters, and placed on a wide shelf in the monks' lavatorium or washing place. There was far more space in which to spread, and pots of green plants were incorporated in the arrangement most successfully. They made a fine display which filled the alcove. There are more examples of the use of pot-grown plants in Chapter 9, Winter Decorations.

THE CLOISTERS – NORTH SIDE

Height overall: 80in (2.03m)
Width overall: 80in (2.03m)

Under the Royal Coat of Arms; The alstromerias shown at their best with their colours blending with Elizabeth I's arms. Although 80x80in in size it looks quite small placed between the Monks' door and the Prior's door on the north side of the cloisters where many visitors walk past it.

Mechanics	Large tub, 12in (30cm) wide at the bottom, 14in (35cm) across the top and 7in (18cm) deep, oasis and wire netting.
Foliage	*Buxus sempervirens* 'Aurea', Golden box *Foeniculum vulgare,* Fennel *Ligustrum ovalifolium* 'Aureum', Golden privet

Flowers   *Alstroemeria ligtu* hybrids, Peruvian lily
                           Centranthus ruber, Valerian

There are three old stone pillars on this side of the cloisters. They are of uneven height, the middle one being taller, and they stand against the north wall beneath several large painted coats of arms of the families who dined with Queen Elizabeth I when she visited Norwich in the 16th century. The Queen's arms are shown in the accompanying photograph. For this occasion, one arrangement was prepared on the centre column using one of the large green tubs, which were donated to the cathedral after the 1977 Flower Festival. The amount of water they can hold gives them great stability, and removes any worry of displays blowing over. It is possible to make three complimentary arrangements on the columns, and this was last done for the 1987 Festival, 'Flowers in Trinity'. As wind in the cloisters is the main concern, every bit of material is pushed in well, and the result checked carefully to see if there are any insecure pieces which a gust of wind could tear loose.

Attractive long stems of alstromeria were the link between all the cloister decorations, and gave the overall effect a feeling of well planned cohesion. The number of different Alstromeria hybrids, which make excellent cut flowers, is constantly increasing, and there is now a wide range of colours from which to select. In 1987 we chose a colour scheme of light gold to deep copper tones, but we avoided red which can look too dark in the corners. These colours were bright and cheerful against the sombre hue of the stone in the closters, and the overall effect provided a suitable contrast to the more than one hundred arrangements in the cathedral. NAFAS members prepared the interior decorations, and as many consisted of several small arrangements placed together, it enabled a large number of members to participate.

The cloisters present quite a challenge to the decorators. They are considerably more difficult to do than the cathedral's interior, but they are well worth the extra effort needed for special occasions.

I hope this chapter explains how complex some of the work carried out by the Flower Guild can be. Although the events described took place during the Summer, the details apply to any event throughout the year.

5

Wedding Day

number of weddings are held in Norwich Cathedral every year. They range from quite simple ceremonies held in a side chapel to much larger occasions in the nave where many more guests can be seated. The High Altar is the most frequently chosen location, and there can be many variations depending on the bride's requirements. Some are quite happy to have the normal weekly roster flowers, others request simple flowers incorporating certain colours, and a few require larger, more formal ceremonies with decorated pews and extra arrangements placed to suit the type of service.

1988 saw a very wide selection, starting with a wedding at the High Altar in Lent during the week before Easter. Permission was granted to have flowers in the sanctuary and the presbytery, but they had to be removed before the Sunday services. The flowers were so arranged that they could be taken out easily, and carried to the Great Hospital, a nearby home for the elderly. Two arrangements were prepared, a simple small pedestal was used in the sanctuary instead of the usual wrought iron stand, and the finished bowl of flowers was kept to a reasonable size. A second vase, containing flowers to compliment the brides-maid's dress, was placed at the top of the presbytery steps.

For a more formal wedding, nearly all the flowers were purchased from a florist in order to be absolutely sure we had everything required by the bride and her mother. The fronts of the pews in the presbytery were decorated, and extra vases were placed at the crossing, the south door, and the top of the presbytery steps. A definite colour scheme, requested by the bride's mother, and discussed several weeks before, was used throughout the decorating. An agreed budget was placed with a local nursery well in advance, and the flowers specified. The colours ranged from white, cream, apricot and peach to gold, and were not the easiest choice for a wet July, but everything was delivered correctly, except that we had to pick out the right colours from the mixed sweet peas. We were also fortunate in obtaining some reasonably priced longifloriums from the nursery, and used these at the High Altar, because these beautiful and impressive flowers added so much to the overall effect. A predecessor of mine, remarking on the addition of a few exceptional blooms, used to say, 'It adds a bit of class.' A few outstanding flowers are more than sufficient, and caution should always be advised, because too many can ruin the desired effect.

It is always a pleasure to be able to work with a selection of good quality blooms, bearing in mind that for the most part we have to make use of whatever is available. The foliage is usually supplied by those members of the Flower Guild who are helping prepare the wedding decorations. The committee member on duty usually asks some of the other members to help, because the increased workload caused by a wedding is far too much for one person to undertake alone.

Most brides or their mothers discuss the preparations, decide what they would

Summer garden flowers were chosen for a wedding held at the cathedral's east end in July. The two troughs can be seen in the foreground with the pew front decorations and the main pedestal arrangements of silver, white and coral pink.

like to have, and how much they are prepared to spend. The cost of course dictates how many commercially grown blooms can be purchased. Ordering the flowers is usually undertaken by the Guild, and while this ensures that we know what we will be using, it also means that we have the responsibility of collecting and looking after them.

As an example to illustrate as many facets as possible, I have chosen a July wedding when Debbie, one of the Dean's daughters, married Peter, a verger, making the occasion a truly cathedral event. They chose mixed summer flowers, mainly garden, with a few scented ones in the presbytery decorations, and the colours, although mixed, were to be principally white and cream, with a touch of coral pink and soft yellow. Bright sugary pinks were to be avoided. As the reception was planned in a marquee on the Deanery lawn, we were also asked to decorate the entrance and interior.

I am convinced that these weddings, requiring a varied and informal effect using garden flowers, are the most difficult occasions we undertake. They cause the most anxiety to everyone involved, because nothing is certain until the last minute. The usual questions about whether certain flowers will be out, if they will last, or if a particular shade will be correct, are asked continually. However, if everything comes right on the day, it is probably the most rewarding work of all. It demonstrates that it is possible to have a beautiful display with a minimum outlay, providing you have a willing team prepared to scour the countryside for the right blooms, and there are enough long suffering garden owners willing to have their flower beds mutilated. As many owners have tried to cut down on garden work, the number of good herbaceous borders has dwindled, resulting in less and less available material. My advice is to attempt an event in this manner, but not too often!

The most frequent error made with wedding decorations is that they are often far too lavish, and dominate the occasion. The bride can too easily find herself competing with a mini-flower festival, and it must be remembered that the flowers are there to compliment her day, not to detract from the religious ceremony. There is simply no need to fill every nook and cranny or each ledge and corner in order to achieve a memorable effect. If the arrangements are placed to draw the eyes towards the altar, and a special display is positioned near the spot where the marriage takes place, the rest is secondary. A good bold arrangement at the entrance will create an excellent first impression, and sets the scene for the whole event. The bride's mother should consider what the interior will look like when all the ladies attending the wedding are wearing hats, obscuring anything small or placed too low. This last point does not apply to Norwich Cathedral because the presbytery pews face each other allowing most of the guests an unhindered view of the decorations.

The illustration shows a general view of the presbytery and sanctuary with some of the different types of wedding decorations which I will describe briefly. This wedding coincided with the Founder's Day celebrations held on the Friday at 10am. Herbert de Losinga, the founder, died on the 22nd July 1119, and was buried in front of the High Altar. Candles have been lit around his tomb. Flower arrangements for the Saturday are normally prepared on Friday morning, but this would have disrupted the service. Consequently, it was decided to begin work on the High Altar on Thursday, after collecting the flowers from the nursery. The arrangement at the north-west corner of the crossing was prepared by a member starting at 8.30am to give her time to finish and clear up in time. The troughs were prepared, put in place, and some of the foliage added before the service, then everyone involved retired to the Deanery and the marquee, returning afterwards to finish the arrangements. This type of problem can occur frequently in a busy cathedral.

FOREGROUND TROUGHS

Height overall: 32in (81cm)
Length overall: 62in (157.5cm)

Mechanics	Plastic window boxes filled with oasis and covered with wire netting
Flowers	Carnations, spray Dahlias Freesias *Gypsophila paniculata*, Baby's breath *Helichrysum splendidum*, Everlasting *Ornithogalum thyrsoides*, Chincherinchees Roses, pale yellow *Senecio maritima*, syn. *Cineraria maritima*, Sea ragwort *Senecio Przewalskii*, The Rocket
Foliage	*Cotoneaster franchetii* *Eucalyptus globulus*, Blue gum *Hosta sieboldiana*, Plantain lily *Sambucus racemosa* 'Plumosa Aurea', Golden elder

These simple but effective decorations are versatile, can easily be moved if required, and can also be comparatively quickly prepared. Smaller troughs can be used to good effect if you need to economise. They act as a focal point at the altar, their position flanks the bridal party, and compliments the colours of the bridesmaids' bouquets. The objective was to include some scented flowers, so roses, freesias and spray carnations were ordered to be sure of success. If the marriage takes place at the sanctuary, the troughs are placed closer, in front of the first two pews nearest the altar rail. Whilst preparing for one wedding, the decorator working near the south door was approached by a visitor who asked if a scent spray had been used! Stocks were the source of the perfume in that instance.

PEW FRONTS

Diameter:	18in (46cm)
Mechanics	Deep saucer Quarter block of well soaked oasis covered with small mesh wire netting, wired to the pew
Flowers	Carnations, spray Freesias *Gypsophila paniculata,* Baby's breath
Foliage	*Buxus sempervirens,* Common box *Cryptomeria japonica,* Japanese cedar

This pew front arrangement, made with colours and materials that blend in with the overall effect, is a neat compact addition to the decorations. It is essential to keep the flowers well sprayed, because they cannot be watered when hanging in position. Providing it is not too hot they should last for a few days.

THE HIGH ALTAR

Overall height:	77in (1.95m)
Overall width:	88in (2.23m)
Mechanics	Wrought iron stand and copper urn Oasis and wire netting
Flowers	*Alstromerias ligtu* hybrids, Peruvian lily *Alchemilla mollis,* Lady's mantle *Chrysanthemum frutescens* 'Marguerite' Carnations, cream and peach spray Gladioli, white Gladioli, pale pink
Foliage	Cotoneaster *Eucalyptus globulus,* Blue gum *Senecio maritima,* syn. *Cineraria maritima,* Sea ragwort *Tilia europea,* European lime *Weigela praecox* 'Variegata', Variegated weigela

The lime trees were in flower at the beginning of July, just ready to be stripped, and as it was a special occasion we decided to prepare some. All the leaves have to be removed, a tedious job which cannot be hurried, but the effect is worthwhile. The finished result is an unusual light green shade which is most attractive. One of our members conveniently had a eucalyptus tree which needed heavy pruning, and the grey branches enhanced the white flowers. White could otherwise have become the dominating focal point of the arrangement, but the grey softened the effect.

A beehive arrangement was placed at the top of the presbytery steps on the north side, close to the pulpit. The design was adapted from an idea used by the ladies of the Washington Cathedral Altar Guild, and a few years ago a party of them visited our cathedral. They kindly sent us a copy of the excellent book *Homage Through Flowers* by Sandra S. Hynson as a memento. The American style of flower arranging is more lavish than ours, but the sentiments to which they adhere are similar.

A BEEHIVE

Overall height: 44in (112cm)
Overall width: 47in (119cm)

Mechanics	Small wooden pedestal
	Washing-up bowl
	Hanging basket
	Oasis
Flowers	Carnations, cream spray
	Carnations, dark and pale salmon spray
	Freesias, yellow
	Gladioli, small white butterfly
	Gypsophila paniculata, Baby's breath
Foliage	*Buxus sempervirens,* Common box

The original American beehive is depicted on a shallow saucer base, but I have found a washing-up bowl an improvement because it holds plenty of water, prevents the oasis drying out, and makes the arrangement last much longer. A plain wire hanging basket with a small mesh is upturned over the oasis, and wired onto the bowl.

This round arrangement can be viewed from all sides. It is more formal than the other decorations prepared for the occasion. The upturned hanging basket was covered with foliage, and the long drooping branches of box with its fine leaves were placed around the base. The Gypsophila or Baby's breath was next placed all over the dome, and the flowers were then systematically added until the surface was covered. As the interior is filled with oasis it is a simple task to place each flower exactly where you require. The perennial *Gypsophila paniculata* is preferable to the annual *G. elegans*, but do make sure you avoid weather damaged material. The finished beehive has a light airy appearance, and its colours compliment the bridesmaids' dresses and bouquets.

The principal arrangements are now completed. There were also displays where the transepts cross in the north-west corner, and at the south door where most of the guests entered. Mixed garden flowers with a few gladioli were used on the pedestal by the entrance. The July weather had been blustery and wet, and we found that most of the material we had hoped to acquire had been badly battered, much of it completely flattened, and unfit for our use. Even when it was possible to make use of garden flowers they were not in a condition to last many days. The problem of how best to divide the available material as well as that purchased from the nursery had to be settled. It was decided to put the long lasting blooms in the cathedral for the enjoyment of the many seasonal tourists and the Sunday congregations, while the remaining flowers were sent over to the marquee where their limited life would not be a problem.

At Norwich we are sometimes criticised for the size of our arrangements, but I am sure that in most cases, if our critics saw the flowers in the context of the occasions for which they are designed, they would appreciate why such large proportions are necessary. Wedding arrangements, for example, are intended to be seen when all the guests are in place, not when the building is empty. Our arrangements in the several chapels are no bigger than those found in the average parish church.

The next illustrations help to explain how the marquee was decorated and, in detail, how the hanging baskets were transformed into floral balls. The broom handles, supporting a white rope slung between them, were used as markers to guide the guests to the entrance, and alongside a bank to prevent anyone slipping. The wooden handles were painted a very pale green, and each was set in concrete poured into either an old flower pot or a mould. They were still not sufficiently steady to stand on a lawn or an uneven surface, so were placed in some of the big green plastic tubs, and made firm with damp sand. This has the added advantage that if someone knocks into one, they do not hurt themselves. They are also reasonably weatherproof, and ideal for standing outside. Their decoration was planned with this in mind, and it did in fact rain in the afternoon.

A block of well soaked oasis was pushed onto the top of each broom handle, secured by wrapping wire netting around it, and then by wiring the netting together under the block. The pale green handle had complimentary white ribbon wound round it from the wire netting to the concrete. In order to save flowers, and because they had to stand outside, the tops were covered with Japanese cedar, box and young tips of *Chamaecyparis pisifera* 'Squarrosa', Sawara cypress, which had all been cut into 6in (15.25cm) lengths. A few bits of *Hypericum calycinum*, Rose of Sharon, were added to the *Alchemilla mollis* with the stripped lime and *Daucus carota*, wild carrot, used to break up the plain green appearance. Many variations can be achieved with these simple broom handles

Left: Decorated broom sticks; the material being applied to completely cover the soaked oasis which has been wrapped in wire netting.

Right: White ribbon adds the bridal touch. It is attached to the wire netting at the top and wound round the pale green painted stick.

---

using either entirely flowers or a combination of foliage and flowers. They can be made to look particularly attractive at Christmas by using both plain and variegated holly, some other foliage and a few artificial flowers. Size can be varied according to where they are to stand. A half block of oasis will be sufficient in some places, but the whole block retains moisture for much longer.

During the 1987 Flower Festival, six broom handles were used in the cloisters to mark the steps which protrude into the cloister alley. They were needed to prevent visitors tripping or falling over the steps, and were decorated with ribbon around the stems and some foliage, mainly golden evergreens.

THE HANGING BASKETS

Mechanics   Baskets of various sizes can be used providing they are
                    not too large or too heavy.
                    Oasis and wire netting
                    Ropes for suspension

Flowers   *Alstromeria ligtu* hybrids, Peruvian lily
                    Althaea rosea, Hollyhocks

Dahlias, mixed
Roses, mixed

Foliage   *Cryptomeria japonica,* Japanese cedar
Fagus sylvatica, Common beech
Ligustrum ovalifolium 'Aureum', Golden privet

Ordinary wire hanging baskets are used for these decorations and, if they are available, I prefer to use the flat bottomed variety with as fine a mesh as possible to secure the blooms. Three blocks of well soaked oasis should be sufficient with some wire netting stretched over the top. It is extremely difficult to work on a hanging basket if it moves every time a piece of foliage or a flower is pushed into the oasis, or if the wind swings it back and forth, so before starting do anchor the basket to the pole with some string, and also make sure that the ropes for hanging them are secured to the poles. Now that you are ready to start, decide how large you want the finished arrangement to be, and begin with a piece of foliage of the right length. If there are several to be decorated, work on two simultaneously to make sure they match. The illustrated baskets had beech, golden privet, cryptomeria and *Alchemilla mollis* used for their foundations. A variety of flowers were added, alstromerias principally, and some brightly coloured dahlias. A few hollyhocks and roses were added with a little stripped lime to lighten the effect. The finished baskets were about 40in (101cm) in diameter, but they can of course be made much bigger, space permitting, or smaller according to requirements.

Once the flowers are in place, the baskets are ready to be hung. They should not be too high because their effect will be lost if they can only be viewed from a distance or by looking up, but they ought to be at least six or seven feet from the ground to allow the guests to move freely without knocking their heads or damaging the display. Leave one of the lengths of string attached as this will facilitate pulling a basket down to water and spray. Each basket will take at least a gallon of water, but it should be done well before the reception to allow time for excess water to drip, and do make sure the caterers have not placed a table underneath.

It is important to consider the marquee's dimensions before beginning work on the hanging baskets, because their size will be effected by the height, whether or not it is lined with drapes, how many poles there are and the distance between them, and if there is to be artificial lighting. The tent hirers will see that the ropes are put in place for you, and will advise on anything else you should know. The marquee's linings are normally striped in two colours, usually white and either pink, blue or yellow, and this must effect the choice of flowers to avoid a clash. Do ask to see a pattern during the planning stage, because the colours vary and often fade.

On a dull day a lined marquee will appear quite dark. Central lighting is usual, but wall brackets are sometimes fitted. Do be prepared to alter your plans if everything is not as expected. I once went to prepare a simple basket for a 21st

Hanging baskets, suspended at the right level for decorating and with stabilising strings attached, being prepared with well soaked oasis.

The groundwork of foliage taking shape with the tool basket in the foreground.

Some of the flowers being added.

The Big Pull; As they often each weigh over 14lb they need secure fastening to make them safe, but allow for them to be lowered in very hot weather in order to soak and spray them thoroughly.

Baskets in a Marquee; Two hanging baskets prepared entirely with odds and ends from different gardens. Although they required a lot of material, they were bright and cheerful on a rainy day, and as they are simple to construct they can be used in many different locations.

---

birthday party, but on arrival I found a modern framed tent, when I had expected and planned for a conventional marquee with a ridge pole between two uprights. The rather large heavy basket was a problem, to fill it required several blocks of oasis, and the tent hirers had visions of the whole structure collapsing. A solution was found by using a sturdy hollow tree trunk as a pedestal for the basket. It was a most unusual but effective alternative, and stood in full view of the entrance beside the band. I recently saw some huge baskets decorated entirely with *Alchemilla mollis* and privet, and finished with hanging ribbons in the bridal colours. I would like the opportunity to prepare some similar ones using agapanthus instead of ribbons, as these marvellous round blooms, both blue and white, mixed with *Alchemilla mollis,* blend so well together.

TABLE DECORATIONS

Diameter: 8in (20cm)

Mechanics   Round blocks of oasis in small saucers

Flowers   Mixed, including heathers

The table decorations and those on the serving tables were prepared using flowers gathered from several gardens combined with heather from the north Norfolk coast. It is a common mistake to underestimate the amount of material required for these small decorations, because comparatively they use more than the larger ones. Once you start to cut material into small pieces, a lot of waste is created, and

Table decorations as work starts with small blocks of oasis in saucers and quantities of mixed flowers and foliage.

A hive of activity showing different types of decorations being carried out simultaneously.

you will be surprised by the quantity used. It is also wise not to underestimate the time it takes to complete a large number of table centres, or the time involved in collecting the material. However, much of the work can be completed at the arranger's home, and then transported to the marquee, although if more than one helper is involved it is important to make sure they know what is required, and produce similar decorations. In order to economise on flowers, margarine pots can be used with a block of oasis and, depending on what is in season, wire netting with a few pebbles to add weight and steady the display can be used for soft stems.

When the reception drew to a close at a wedding I attended recently, some of the guests were seen leaving with the table pieces, taking them as charming mementoes of the day. As the occasion was celebrated by a dinner dance the table decorations were of particular importance, and were larger and higher than usual.

The illustration shows several *Campanula pyramidalis,* chimney flowers, in pots which were grouped together to compliment the cake cutting ceremony. Two weeks later they were still in bloom, and standing in the cathedral near the Friends' table. They travelled, packed with tissue paper supporting their heads and placed in an open-ended flower box, flat in the back of an estate car. Care was taken to stabilise the flower pots to prevent any rolling.

The above describes the work involved in preparing a cathedral wedding followed by a reception in a marquee. Three full days were needed for the main preparations, and most weddings require the same time, because so much effort is involved just fetching and carrying. At this point we will leave the Summer flowers and turn to the early Autumn.

Chrysanthemums, mainly spray varieties, growing with netting support which moves upwards as the plants develop. This method cuts out the need for continual staking and tieing, and greatly facilitates picking.

The nave from the triforium's west end showing most of the RAF's flowers including the pair
at the screen and the pairs of matching pedestals. They made a glorious colourful display when
viewed from the nave's west end.

6

A Time of Thanksgiving

uring the early Autumn, a time of plenty and thanksgiving, both foliage and blooms produce bright colours. Two separate weeks are covered in this chapter; the Royal Air Force's annual service to commemorate the Battle of Britain was held in mid-September, and during the second week of October a thanksgiving service for the Arts and another wedding were held in the cathedral. The Battle of Britain service took place in the nave, while the October events were held in the east end; the thanksgiving service at the Crossing Altar and the wedding at the High Altar. These two events included a great variety of decorations from the opulent to the restrained.

During September and October outdoor chrysanthemums and dahlias are at their best. Chrysanthemums will last for up to three weeks providing they are used soon after cutting, but if they are to retain their fresh appearance and to avoid waste, it is essential that a Guild member should check the arrangements regularly to remove any dead flowers and leaves. It is amazing how a few replacements will completely transform a tired arrangement into a fresh display. I would recommend that the dead material is cut out rather than pulled to avoid the risk of a collapse. This important job is often done by the waterers, and, although it may not be very interesting, it is a great contribution to the budget and ensures that visitors are not greeted by the sight of dead and dying flowers. Vases that are forgotten or neglected look so sad, and detract from the very building which they were intended to enhance. Anyone undertaking this work should not underestimate the time it involves, often as long as preparing the arrangements afresh.

The annual Battle of Britain Service in Norwich Cathedral is a major occasion for decorating the nave, and a day when the Flower Guild members take a back seat to the RAF wives. It is their 'big day' and planning takes several weeks. RAF wives are seldom available for more than two consecutive years, thus ensuring that there will always be a large percentage of novice arrangers. It is possible that for some of them it will be their first experience, not only in a place as large as a cathedral, but in any building requiring pedestal decorations of ample proportions.

A blueprint has evolved over several years enabling the work to be carried out quickly and smoothly. Some years ago a major change took place in the RAF's arrangements; the lady, who had previously donated all the flowers in memory of a relative, died herself. Her death left a gap which has been filled by several of the RAF stations not only donating the purchased flowers but paying for the oasis used in the decorations. The latter is a bonus as it keeps us supplied for several weeks after the event. The timetable for the work begins on the Friday morning before the service when a group of RAF personnel and some of the wives visit the garden of one of the Guild members to cut foliage. As such a large amount is needed it is no small task, and they arrive with a long wheelbase Land Rover and

On the North Side of the Nave; Several of the nave arrangements in lovely autumnal colours achieved by using mainly chrysanthemums.

Flowers

Chrysanthemums, large decorative, bronze and copper with gold and white
Double spray, orange, yellow and white
Single spray, red and bronze
Dahlias, red and copper
Gladioli, red, yellow and white

Foliage

Acer platanoides, Copper maple
x Cupressocyparis leylandii, Leyland Cypress
Fagus sylvatica, Common Beech
Ligustrum ovalifolium 'Aureum', Golden privet
Prunus cerasifera 'Pissardii', Myrobalan
Thuja plicata 'Aureovariegata', Western red cedar

several large plastic dustbins. The bins are filled, and their number and depth ensures that the material cut is of both the right size and quantity for the cathedral. RAF stations are not noted for having a good supply of bushes to hack at.

The next step, the same day, is to visit the cathedral where they condition the foliage, and prepare for the flowers' arrival. The oasis is soaked for at least two hours to absorb water fully, and the vases are then prepared. Extra wire netting is usually needed, and some of the men set about the task of rigging up the bowls. They also do all the heavy lifting, and carrying the pedestals and containers to their allotted places. This preparatory work leaves everything ready and in place for an early start on the Saturday morning. This is one week in the year when the flowers are prepared on a Saturday because so many of the wives work from Monday to Friday.

The photographs show that the decorations vary considerably, but the overall appearance achieved was the result of a well thought out co-ordinated effort. The 'Flight of RAF Wives' (a collective description suggested by an ex-WAAF, which is really too good to omit) appear on Saturday morning. They start by collecting their foliage and blooms, then quickly set to work, knowing in advance where they will be in the cathedral. The first timers take a little longer to begin than those who prepared the decorations the previous year, but it is always surprising how well and efficiently the novices tackle the work, and they do achieve great satisfaction from the finished decorations. They will copy the person on the opposite side of the nave, or will ask for advice from anyone who happens to be close at hand. Their cheerful and enthusiastic co-operation is an example for others, and an inspiration for those prepared to have a go.

Two weeks after the RAF service, some of the blooms were still fresh enough to be in use thanks to the careful watering carried out by the RAF during the week following their service. This is a bonus for the regular waterers as there is a lot of extra work required. Some of the novice arrangers are inclined to put too much oasis in the bowls, presumably because they are afraid of the flowers falling out, with the result that it dries out, especially when not enough room is left to pour the water into the container. The water levels were checked every day during the following week, but in spite of this attention some still dried out. It was decided that the photographer should take most of the shots from the triforium in order to show the overall effect to best advantage, especially from the west end.

The decorations from the nave's east end working towards the west end included:

Nave Screen	– Two wall brackets
Altar, north side	– Tall pedestal
Altar, south side	– RAF emblem
Chancellor Spencer's tomb	– Trough
Nave	– Pair of pedestals
The Parsley tomb	– Trough
Nave	– Pair of pedestals

West end — Pedestal
West end (behind the seating) — Two large tubs on the floor

This selection produced a good overall effect, and has progressed a great deal from the days when twenty-four assorted vases and bowls were dotted all over the place. They were stuffed with blooms without any additional foliage, and the vases on pedestals were so small they could only be seen by someone sitting next to them. The foliage has transformed the entire operation into a very special occasion for all those who take part, and we are very grateful to the Royal Air Force for their generosity.

The accompanying photograph shows the well known Wings emblem of the RAF created with flowers and laurel leaves. The wings were cut out of hardboard, then dry oasis was placed on the board and cut to its shape before

The RAF's Wings emblem was created with flowers and laurel leaves for the Battle of Britain annual service of remembrance.

All the flowers in the nave were prepared by the RAF wives. An arrangement on Chancellor Spencer's tomb and one of the pedestals are shown viewed from the triforium.

removing it in sections like a jigsaw to be soaked. Hooks were stuck into the board to support the oasis which, when finally attached, was ready to take the flowers and leaves. The laurel leaves were individually pinned in position, a slow job, but one which looks most effective when completed. The red, white and blue rings were created with carnations, and some of the white blooms were sprayed with blue dye. A painted crown surmounts the wings, and when the display was finished it was lifted onto a metal stand, and the red, white and blue drapes attached *in situ* to cover the metal. The wings were a great attraction for the RAF personnel attending the remembrance service.

The beginning of October was extremely busy, and it was a problem to arrange everything so that it blended together. It saw the week of the thanksgiving service which was to take place at the Crossing Altar. The harvest theme was introduced into the nave decorations, as the main topic of the service was to be the Arts, and there was also the wedding at the east end. After much

Dahlias for the Thanksgiving Service; These bright and cheerful flowers were grown in one of the Close gardens and made a fitting splash of colour at the Nave Altar.

deliberation over the problem of co-ordination, we decided to do the following: five candlesticks were to feature at the Arts' service, one to be placed at each of the crossing's four corners and a fifth larger one to stand at the back of the altar in front of the presbytery steps. These candlesticks could not be positioned until after the wedding and Saturday's evensong, so we agreed that simple chaplets of greenery would be the solution, and the Vergers would be able to put them onto the candlesticks. Five ring moulds were therefore filled with well soaked oasis, and then covered with small bits of *Thuja plicata* 'Aureovariegata', Western red cedar, and a few pieces of *Chamaecyparis obtusa* 'Crippsii', Hinoka cypress. These pretty chaplets were the right shade of bright green to show up well, and scrolls were attached to each candlestick for each of the arts.

The photograph of the harvest produce on Chancellor Spencer's tomb illustrates the decorative straw cross hung from a 2x2in (5x5cm) wooden upright, 5ft (1.53m) tall, which was fixed securely in a concrete block. The cross has been worked on a wooden base covered with red velvet on which the straw shows up well. The frame was made of 2.5x1in (6.5x2.5cm) for the upright, and 1.5x0.5in (4x1.2cm) for the cross bar. The finished cross is approximately 5x3ft (1.5x0.9m). Wheat and barley sheaves were placed at the foot of the cross, and there was a great assortment of agricultural and horticultural produce. The apples were by courtesy of the local Fruit Growers Association, and a lovely harvest loaf was baked specially for the occasion.

On the opposite side of the Nave Altar, and placed on one of the tall wooden pedestals, was a large arrangement of dahlias and mixed Autumn foliage which completed the harvest theme.

THE NAVE ALTAR – NORTH SIDE

Materials   Pedestal, tall wooden
          Copper urn

Foliage   *Cotoneaster lacteus*
          Fagus sylvatica, Common beech
          Fagus sylvatica 'Riversii', Purple beech
          Ligustrum ovalifolium 'Aureum', Golden privet
          Molucella laevis, Bells of Ireland
          Senecio maritima, syn. *Cineraria maritima*, Sea Ragwort

Flowers   Dahlias, mixed colours
          Fuchsia, hardy

This was a BIG, BOLD and BRIGHT arrangement which showed up extremely well in the nave, as the area at the east end close to the organ is very dark. All the dahlias came from a garden in the Close which was appropriate for a thanksgiving service in the cathedral.

Left: The Beehive; Detail of work on this bridal arrangement showing the base of Leylandii.

Right: Fixing the five foot straw cross to the upright to become the focal point of the harvest display.

The wedding held at the High Altar was that of Mr Munro Webster to Dr Premila Thangaraj, his bride from Madras. Mr. Webster's father was Dean of Norwich Cathedral from 1970 to 1978. The flowers at the High Altar were white, and a beehive arrangement was placed on the presbytery's south side in front of Bishop Goldwell's tomb, 1499, near the steps, as shown in the accompanying photograph.

A BEEHIVE

Materials	Bowl, 10in (25.5cm) diameter
	Hanging basket, 10in (25.5cm) diameter
Foliage	x *Cupressocyparis leylandii*, Leyland cypress
	Hedera colchica 'Variegata', Variegated ivy
Flowers	Chrysanthemums, spray varieties
	'Primrose Salter'
	'Golden Salter'
	'Salmon Susan Rowe'
	Lilies, deep orange

Lilies for an Indian Bride; This beehive arrangement of chrysanthemums on a base of conifers was completed by adding the lilies to match the bride's bouquet.

An Abundance of Harvest Produce; A wide range of produce from rural Norfolk was displayed on Chancellor Spencer's tomb on the south side of the Nave Altar for the thanksgiving service.

I found a pile of freshly cut Leyland cypress hedge trimmings, covered the upturned basket with them, and then added a few pieces of ivy to hang down over the lower edge. The dark foliage was a good background for the brightly coloured lilies and chrysanthemums. Most of the blooms were secondary ones, a lot smaller than the main crop, and ideal for this use. This decoration is a good example of what can produced with inexpensive flowers, and it has the added benefit that as the flowers are so securely in place the display can easily be moved.

The photograph shows chrysanthemums growing, held up by netting 36in (0.9m) wide with a 5in (12.7cm) mesh, which is attached to several uprights and raised throughout the summer as the plants grow. This simple method avoids all the time consuming tying and staking.

The low loading trolley which is invaluable for carting the produce for the harvest display and a great help throughout the year.

There were two more pedestals in the south transept; the one near the south door was placed to welcome the wedding guests, and the other at the north-west corner had white and copper chrysanthemums which blended in with the wedding and the thanksgiving service.

THE SOUTH DOOR PEDESTAL

Materials   Pedestal, adjustable iron
Bowl, copper urn

Foliage   *Cotoneaster lacteus*
Fagus sylvatica, Common beech

Flowers   Chrysanthemums, spray varieties
'White Margaret'
'Fleet Margaret'
'Bronze Margaret'
'Copper Margaret'
Peach, single spray
Lilies, light orange

The cotoneaster was particularly useful, because it has very graceful branches which broke up the more solid looking dahlias and chrysanthemums in two of the arrangements described in this chapter.

From east to west, we worked with white at the High Altar and bright reds in the nave, but the colours blended well producing a co-ordinated effect. I hope this demonstrates that such a display can be achieved with a little planning, and providing it is done in advance it can prevent much wasted effort. I would recommend to anyone who has the job of organising the flowers, whether in a cathedral or a small village church, to consider how to achieve the best overall display. An assortment of jugs and vases full of dried up flowers, often placed on the floor near a tomb, does not look very welcoming. I heard one such collection described as boring, and I am afraid such a description said it all. So, do please consider where the flowers can be placed for them to give of their best.

7

The Advent Ring

he Friday before Advent Sunday marks the end of the season for the Flower Guild and the start of the Church year. It is the day when all the flowers are removed, and the vases and pedestals taken away then cleaned and stored in preparation for Christmas. It is another time consuming job which has to be done, even if it is not one of the tasks which gives much pleasure to the committee member whose lot it is to clear up. When nothing remains, the Advent ring, a large papier mâché circle, is brought out of storage, and placed at the crossing. It is from this spot that it will be hung from chains and suspended from the bell tower. Its dimensions are as follows:

Ring diameter:	5ft (1.52m) diameter
Height:	8ft 6in (2.65m) from the ground when suspended 101.5ft (31m) from the bell tower hatch
Candles	18in (45cm) tall, 2.25in (6cm) diameter
Green baubles	Matt finish, 2in (5cm) diameter
Material for the foundation	Wire netting, 1in (2.5cm) mesh
	Newspapers
	4 Plastic flower holders on stems with screw-on bases
	Paste
	Spray paint, matt black
	Pipe, metal
	Thin wire for tying greenery and attaching baubles
Foliage	*Hedera helix*, Common ivy, English ivy (US)
	Hedera colchica 'Variegata', Ivy
	Ilex aquifolium 'Silver Queen', Variegated holly

The ring was constructed on a wire netting base, which was formed by rolling a length of the wire netting into a tubular shape, then bending it into a circle about 5ft (1.5m) in diameter. In order that the right dimensions would be achieved, the ring was carefully marked out with tailor's chalk on the Deanery's sitting room carpet. A piece of string was held in place in the centre and the chalk, attached to the opposite end, was used to mark the circle and form the pattern. The committee ladies spent an enjoyable morning tearing newspaper into strips about 2x8in (5x20cm) long to make the papier mâché, then after dipping them in paste they stuck the paper to the netting. The paste should be stiffer than when used for wallpapering, and each layer should be allowed to dry before the next is applied. Hair driers were used to speed up the process, although it proved too much for

Fixing the greenery to the Advent Ring while it hangs a few inches above the floor in the crossing.

The Vergers, wearing safety climbing harnesses, ready to go up to the bell tower to hoist the ring to the required height.

one elderly drier and the ensuing sparks had to be extinguished quickly! Three layers were applied, and once it was thoroughly dry, the surface was sprayed with matt black paint which gave the appearance of wrought iron without the weight.

Four plastic flower holders on stems were attached through the netting at equal intervals. The screw-on bases of these holders can be detached allowing them to be pushed through the mesh, then secured firmly. Extra strengthening papier mâché was then worked around the stems.

The main problem with this project was deciding how to attach the very heavy 18in (45cm) candles securely and safely. The flower holders catch the hot wax before it can damage the main ring, but much more support was needed. We tried pushing the candles into oasis but this proved completely inadequate, and damp from the oasis softened the papier mâché. Eventually we used sections of metal pipe which provided good firm sleeves once they were glued into position using 'Araldite'. The process could not be rushed as time had to be allowed for the glue to set firm. The accompanying photographs were taken when the ring was being decorated for the second year by which time most of the gremlins had been foreseen and overcome. The ring was moved from the crossing into the nave for the main Christmas services, so that it could be enjoyed by a greater number of people.

The greenery attached to the ring represents life at a time of the year when all outside growth is dormant. Unfortunately it does become rather dry, and should be removed at least once during Advent. Some rings have twelve fir cones to represent the months plus four bows for the seasons. The four candles, one for each Sunday in Advent, are lit one by one until all are alight together on the fourth Sunday. Rings that are placed on tables often have central candles to represent the light of Christ, and these are lit on Christmas Day. Small individual rings can be made for the Sunday school children to take home. At Norwich we use purple candles for Advent and red ones for Christmas.

Hoisting the ring aloft from the bell tower is entirely the work of the Vergers. The tower's roof is 110ft (33m) above the floor, so climbing harnesses are put on for safety. They open the hatch in the bell tower from which they lower the rope which is already on a block and pulley. The rope is then attached to chains wired to the ring, and it is first raised about 18in (45cm) off the floor for the final decorating to take place, as illustrated. Finally it is suspended about 8½ft (2.6m) above the floor near the Crossing Altar. This is an occasion when the tool basket proves invaluable, because the needs are endless, and there is no knowing what will be required. Wire of all gauges and lengths is needed for tying on the greenery and baubles; and glue, secateurs and scissors are constantly required. We use nylon fishing line to hold the ring steady when it is raised, and the lines are taken up to the triforium and secured to prevent any swaying. A good firm pair of steps is most important for fixing the heavy candles into their holders.

The Advent Ring does not look very high, but it still tends to sway even with the lines attached, forcing the decorator to lean over to hold it steady. The illustrations show how some of the work was carried out, and while it was being

Left: More details of the ring being decorated. Note the candleholder.

Right: The ring suspended at the correct level. The Canon Treasurer fixing the candles or is he trying to find the quickest way to heaven?

---

prepared a steady stream of curious visitors passed by to see what we were doing. It certainly served to focus attention on the Advent season.

After Advent, the ring was moved from its position in the crossing to the nave, approximately in the centre in line with the Parsley tomb on the north side, as illustrated in Chapter 8. The greenery was removed and replaced with fresh material, in this case Norway spruce and bits of Leyland cypress. The candles were replaced by bright red ones, and the baubles were also changed to red. The new decoration was finished with several lengths of ivy, and it made a very attractive centre piece in the nave, blending well with the four baskets used as supporting arrangements.

The photographs show how high it is, and the overall size in relationship to both the altars at the crossing and in the nave.

The illustration of the small ring shows a traditional Danish one (*Advents krans*) decorated in their red and white national colours and complete with red bows. It has a background of *Picea glauca,* white spruce, and is quite acceptable to our English tradition of never using red or white on their own. A ring of this size, from 10in (25cm) to 12in (30cm) in diameter, with 1 ½in (4cm) candles, and an overall height of 3in (8cm) can be used in any church, and is particularly popular with children.

Providing the greenery is kept moist the endless work of replacing dried out

The Advent Ring; This five foot diameter ring hangs from the bell tower at the crossing during the Advent season, and is just low enough for the candles to be lit from ground level.

material will be minimised, because a week over the hot pipes is as long as any fresh foliage will last, especially when there is no water or oasis involved.

Advents Krans; A traditional Danish ring of a suitable size for displaying in any building.

Collecting the Christmas Trees; The Sacrist loading the trees onto a lorry before transporting them to the cathedral in time for the carol services.

8

Christmas Celebrations

hristmas preparations start early at Norwich Cathedral when the trees arrive in time for the first of the many carol services held each year. Several schools are among the different organisations which make use of the excellent facilities provided by the cathedral, good acoustics, a superb organ, warmth and the room to seat several hundred people.

The Vergers collect the donated trees from an estate near Norwich after they have been carefully chosen for their size and shape. Those that are to stand in pairs are selected to match each other, and in some cases, where space has to be considered, a tree with tight upward facing branches is preferable to one with outward spreading foliage. The size and number required is planned in advance to allow time for felling in case of inclement weather. There is usually one 16-18ft (5-5.5m) tree to stand in the west end, two in the nave about 12-14ft (3.6-4.2m) high, and sometimes two smaller ones are placed at the east end depending on what other decorations have been planned.

The Vergers have the task of decorating the trees with large multi-coloured baubles because these are hung mainly for the schools' benefit, and are not part of the Flower Guild's work. Personally I am relieved that we do not have to do the job as I would hate to perch at the top of such tall steps. The trees are fixed into proper supports, metal tripods similar to those supplied by garden centres for household trees. They were originally placed in barrels, but these were more difficult to fix securely.

In 1988 it was decided to make some changes in the arrangements as the Nave Altar was to be in the forward position for the Christmas services, and the large sculpture of the Holy Family placed in the nave in front of the screen. A decorated tree did not seem to blend in with the group, so we decided to take drastic action. After the carol services, one of the trees had its baubles removed, and was then cut down to a height suitable to form a background to the Holy Family. Some branches of Norwegian spruce and a small arrangement of flowers were also placed adjacent to the sculpture. This provides yet another example of the invaluable help given to us by the Vergers, but it is not a procedure I would wish to repeat, because with a little foresight we could have planned the whole operation, and put a tree of the correct proportions in place from the start. The other tree, from the nave's screen end, was removed and taken to the opposite end where it was placed at the north-west side of the magnificent West Door. It thus formed a pair, although not matching. We all thought that this was an improvement on the previous location of the trees.

Having dealt with the trees in the nave, the way was clear to begin decorating in time for the cathedral's own carol services. All the members of The Flower Guild Committee arrived on the 20th December bringing as much material as each could transport. They all knew in advance where they were to start and what

Christmas in the Nave; The ring was moved into the centre of the nave and decorated to match the rest of the Christmas decorations. It is shown flanked by the hanging baskets which made this a very festive scene.

they had to do, so the work began without delay.

The member in charge of hanging the eight baskets was amongst the first to arrive, having previously taken them home to attach the chains securely. This is an important task because they are very heavy when filled with wet oasis, and it would hardly do for one of them to fall on a member of the congregation. The oasis was then well soaked and placed in the baskets which were first lined with polythene in order to stop too much dripping. It was then necessary to enlist the Vergers' help to suspend the baskets from the triforium at intervals along the nave. This is accomplished by attaching long chains to the smaller ones already on

A Welcome at the West End; To create an overall effect poinsettias were used as the highlights in this large tub of holly as they go so well with the hanging baskets suspended from the triforium.

the baskets plus stout rope with which to lower and raise them. All the baskets are first left hanging at a convenient height at which they can be decorated, about four feet from the floor. Two lengths of twine are tied to each basket and then to the chairs to keep movement to a minimum in the same way that we carried out the work in the marquee.

Eight baskets were decorated in 1988, and the amount of material needed must not be underestimated, because far more is used than for pedestal arrangements. However, they are visible to a larger number of people and are well out of the way from any interference. We do try and position them where they will be well lit and thus seen to their greatest advantage. The Advent ring, which by then had been moved into the nave, also dictated where the baskets should hang, because they were intended to be part of a group around the ring without overshadowing it. We decided to hang the baskets within the arches in front of and behind the ring, but not in the two closest to it.

THE HANGING BASKETS

Mechanics 12in (30.5cm) diameter wire hanging baskets
Suspension chains: 3 from the basket
1 from the triforium
Oasis, three blocks for each basket (two are suitable for smaller decorations)
Polythene for lining the baskets

Foliage *Buxus sempervirens,* Common box
Cryptomeria japonica. Japanese cedar
x *Cupressocyparis* leylandii, Leyland cypress
Ilex aquifolium 'Silver Queen', Variegated holly
Picea abies, Norwegian spruce
Taxus baccata, English yew

Flowers, Carnations, red silk
   Artificial Ferns, silver artificial foliage
Ferns, gold artificial foliage
Poinsettias, red silk
Ribbons, red and gold (These are easily and quickly made into bows by pulling the draw strings, and they can be folded up, rather like a concertina, and repeatedly used for economy)

As can be seen from the illustrations, the making up follows the same pattern as for the Summer baskets hung in the marquee. The foundation was formed by pushing a lot of mixed foliage into the oasis at all angles in order to make a reasonable shape, neither too tight nor too formal. When the outline was finished,

No apologies for showing more detail of the work on these decorations. Everything has to be pushed in carefully to arrive at the right finished shape.

Ribbons and artificial material are always added when the basic work has been finished to give the display a Christmas look.

the artificial flowers and foliage were similarly added taking into account how they would look under the lights. The bows were finally attached from below enabling them to be seen clearly. Two to each basket were used, and because they reflect the artificial lights they add to the bright cheerful colours which are so much a part of Christmas, enjoyed by both children and adults alike.

When all the baskets were completed, the Vergers pulled them up to the required height, and made sure each one was hung in the centre of an arch. It is essential to have someone on the floor checking the height from several different points to make sure they are all at the correct level.

The baskets are an important feature of the decorations, and are inexpensive to make because so much of the meterial used can be stored for subsequent years. I would always recommend buying the best artificial flowers allowed by your budget, as this is an occasion when quality is preferable to quantity. The baskets are sprayed from above to keep the material fresh for as long as possible because they remain in place until after Epiphany on the 6th January, and usually until the following weekend.

THE WEST DOOR PEDESTAL ARRANGEMENT

Overall height:	75in (190cm)
Overall width:	68in (173cm)
Mechanics	Green tub
	Tall wooden pedestal
	Wire netting
	Oasis
Foliage	*Hedera*, Ivy
	Ilex x altaclarensis 'Golden King', Holly
	Ilex aquifolium 'Silver Queen', Holly
Flowers	*Euphorbia pulcherrima*, Poinsettia, pot-grown
Material	Poinsettias, artificial to add to the display

The pedestal arrangement by the west door was planned as a large and bold display, and a second similar one was placed by the north-west door to welcome visitors. They both blended well with the large Christmas trees at the nave's west end, and were kept fresh by careful watering. Holly is not the easiest shrub to arrange because not only does it have sharp prickles, but it also has a tendency to turn showing the underside of the leaves, and the berries sometimes remain stubbornly hidden from general view. It is important to arrange the foliage in the way it would naturally fall or bend.

Left: Work being carried out on a large pedestal arrangement at the West Door showing the necessity of working from a step-ladder.

Right: The background of mixed greenery taking shape as the large amount of material on the floor diminishes.

The illustrations give some impression of the amount of material required and how it is shaped. Cutting, preparing and then transporting it to the cathedral is the most time consuming part of the decorating. This type of foliage is the most bulky and the most difficult with which we have to contend, and in some years the weather makes its gathering and carriage a real *tour de force*. As the final results are not out of place, and in some cases even look quite small when they are high up in such an enormous building, the visiting public are rarely aware of how much work and effort is involved. I doubt whether many consider from where such vast quantities of foliage materialise.

Due to the magnitude of the task, it really is essential to stop for a break over a welcome cup of coffee and some other refreshments. A picnic in the nave gives us the opportunity to compare progress reports, and to see if there is anything going begging. It is surprising how much quicker and efficiently everyone works after the short interval.

THE NAVE ALTAR

Overall height:	122in (3.1m)
Width at top:	72in (1.8m)
lower section:	58in (1.5m)

Mechanics	Wrought iron stand from the High Altar
	Bowls, various built up from the floor, and secured to the lower part of the stand
	Copper urn which fits into the top
	Oasis
	Wire netting
Foliage	*Hedera*, Ivy
	Ilex aquifolium, Common variegated holly
Flowers	Chrysanthemums, white and bright yellow
	Euphorbia pulcherrima, Poinsettias, pot-grown
Materials	Poinsettias, artificial
	Ribbons

This magnificent and dramatic decoration was prepared from the top section down, filling in the lower part to make the whole display blend together. It was designed to give the impression of being one large display when viewed. One visitor was overheard criticising the use of yellow, but our answer to that response is that we never use red and white on their own, and the arrangement, without the extra bright colours, would not show up well in the nave. It is a clear cut case of having a good reason for doing something slightly different. Every year we find something which could be improved or has not really pleased us, so no two years are alike. There are often events taking place in the cathedral which dictate what decorations are needed. For example, in 1985 we had to prepare extra decorations for the great occasion of the enthronement of Bishop Peter Nott. In 1987 the Midnight Eucharist was televised, and we were forced to work around the camera positions. This event was rather a disappointment to the Flower Guild, as the east end was lit from the ambulatory and the powerful television lighting threw the principle arrangements near the Bishop's throne into silhouette. It has made us aware of the dramatic difference lighting can make.

A 5x2ft (1.5mx61cm) hanging decoration was produced for the south side of the altar. It was constructed on a board with a block of oasis, holly, yew, artificial poinsettias and ribbons which were used to pick up the theme of the north side arrangement. Such decorations can be prepared at home as they are easily transported. This one was hung by wire to a nail already in the stone column, fortunately at exactly the right height required.

At the Nave Altar; This tall decoration was designed to attract attention towards the altar and to be the primary focal point in the nave at Christmas. It was constructed with a mass of greenery, gold and red flowers and a few white ones to show up well in any light.

THE PARSLEY MONUMENT TOMB

Overall width: 33in (84cm)

Mechanics   Small low dish
Oasis
Wire netting

Foliage   *Ilex,* Holly with yellow berries
Ilex, Holly with red berries
Hedera, Ivy

This very low arrangement was placed on the tall tomb to alleviate the bareness of the dark black top. It had to be kept low because there is extra seating behind the tomb which is used during the Christmas services. No-one wants to peer through a mass of branches even if they do have holly berries on them! It does have the added benefit that it is easily kept fresh, as no-one has to climb a ladder to water it.

The Holy Family was placed at the nave's east end on the north side of the screen near the organ loft. A display of white chrysanthemums mixed with silver variegated holly was arranged in the iron bracket on the south side, which showed up well from a distance, and was in keeping with the Virgin and Christ Child. The High Altar can be seen through the arch under the organ, and the three bright decorations at the altar can be seen clearly even without lighting.

Norwich Cathedral has the Bishop's throne in the ancient position behind the High Altar, and there are two troughs on the ledgers on each side of the throne.

TROUGHS

Mechanics   20x5in (50x12.5cm) plastic window boxes
Oasis
Wire netting

Foliage   *Hedera,* Ivy, variegated to cover the steps
Ilex aquifolium 'Silver Queen', Variegated holly
Ilex x altaclarensis 'Golden King', Golden holly
Picea abies, Norwegian spruce

Opposite, Upper Left: The foundation for the spectacular Christmas decoration at the High Altar. A stake, set in concrete, with three equally spaced hanging baskets attached. The bottoms of the baskets have to be cut in order to slot them onto the upright.

Upper Right: The baskets are lined with polythene to help retain moisture in the oasis.

Lower Left: Some of the material required to complete the column.

Lower Right: This massive construction nearing completion. It can be prepared with flowers in the Summer, but doing so would be an expensive luxury.

At the High Altar; This ten foot column was the principal decoration in the sanctuary. The two troughs, either side of the Bishop's throne, containing holly and poinsettias were an integral part of the design for the east end.

Flowers	*Euphorbia pulcherrima,* Poinsettias, pot-grown
Material	Poinsettias, artificial, five in each trough

The holly was placed in the troughs, and the Norwegian spruce pushed in at the back to cut out any light showing through the holly. This must be done to make the whole display show up well. The pot-grown poinsettias are placed centrally, and the artificial ones added on each side.

THE HIGH ALTAR – NORTH SIDE

Overall height:	120in (310cm)
Width, bottom:	68in (173cm)
top:	52in (132cm)

Mechanics	Deep tub 2x2in (5x5cm) wood stake in concrete Three 12in (30.5cm) hanging baskets attached to the upright stake Oasis Polythene lining
Foliage	x *Cupressocyparis leylandii,* Leyland cypress *Ilex aquifolium* 'Silver Queen', Variegated holly *Picea abies,* Norway spruce
Flowers	*Euphorbia pulcherrima,* Poinsettias
Material	Poinsettias, artificial silk and plastic

Another tall decoration, 10ft (3m) high and about 5ft (1.5m) wide which shows up well at all times. The accompanying photographs show how it gradually took shape, working with care to make sure it was filled completely, and could be viewed from as wide an angle as possible. The pot-grown poinsettias were then fixed in position so that they could be seen to their best advantage. Both silk and plastic flowers were used to fill up the tall column. The use of baskets made it possible to insert the foliage at any angle, up or down. The pots were then attached in positions where they would show up well, and could be easily removed for watering which is best done by placing them in washing up bowls to absorb the water through their roots. Most modern composts are better if treated in this manner. While doing this one year I realised how excellent the modern silk poinsettias are; I pulled out one pot to place in the bowl, but the next one I tried to move turned out to be a branch of silk flowers. I did feel rather silly! Although it is always preferable to use fresh plants, the artificial ones can be safely substituted where their position makes watering difficult. The initial cost is about the same as real plants, but they can be washed and then used for several years. They can be stored for use the following Christmas by tying them together and placing them in plastic bags. Most of the artificial branches can easily be split into small sections, which also makes them most versatile and adaptable.

I must stress that anyone attempting this sort of decorating should make sure they have enough material before actually beginning, although when the column illustrated was being prepared a raiding party went into the Close where there are some excellent trees. The cathedral heating does dry out foliage very quickly, but all the decorations which had most of their material in well soaked oasis kept their fresh appearance throughout the Christmas period.

Finally, the last of the Christmas decorations illustrated is appropriately set in one of the chapels.

THE BAUCHON CHAPEL

Overall height: 50in (127cm)
Overall width: 44in (112cm)

Mechanics
Pedestal, wrought iron adjustable
Bowl, 8in (20cm) diameter
Oasis
Wire netting
Two white candles, 16in (40.5cm) tall, 1½in (4cm) thick

Foliage
Ceanothus impressus, Californian lilac, Santa Barbara ceanothus (US)
Cupressus macrocarpa 'Donard Gold', Monterey cypress
Cytisus, Broom
Ilex aquifolium 'Silver Queen', Variegated holly
Mahonia bealei

This display is a simple arrangement designed to stand next to the Madonna (Our Lady of Pity) on the left hand side of the altar. This beautiful statue was donated by Mrs Gribble in memory of her only son Herbert, a young Royal Artillery officer, who died in 1943 while a prisoner of the Japanese. The altar frontal is golden and there are blue hangings within the chapel. The Bauchon Chapel, built in 1330, was restored by the Friends of Norwich Cathedral in 1958, and the flowers are seen at close quarters by the many visitors who walk round the ambulatory. There is very little space behind the wrought iron screen and gates, so a compact formal arrangement fits into this space well. The candles are a festive addition, appropriately placed near the Madonna.

The Bauchon Chapel; Our Lady of Pity looks down on a green and gold arrangement and matching candle which gave the chapel a seasonally festive air.

The Nave at Christmas; The children gazing at the Nativity scene complete this seasonal picture. The hanging baskets along the length of the nave can also be seen.

9

Winter Decorations

Pot-et-Fleur

fter the Epiphany service on the 6th January, it is time to remove the Christmas decorations. Rather than doing this all at once, we prefer to tackle it in two stages. First, we take out all the material which has dried out or withered, and this usually ensures that the main decorations last until the weekend following Epiphany. Then secondly, the main work of removing all the Christmas decorations combined with bringing in fresh material to completely refurbish the arrangements for the period until Lent. We have experimented over several years, and have found that the best solution is that illustrated in the accompanying photographs.

At this time of the year, the weather can cause a number of difficulties, and it is not wise to expect any Guild member to always be able to travel in from the country, especially when some live as far as thirty miles away and many contend with a forty mile round trip. One year several of us were snowed in, when the funeral of one of the Cathedral Canons took place. The lady in charge was unable to drive out of her gate, but she was able to contact another member who struggled into the city, collecting some flowers from the market on her way. Some were frozen, but the stall holder gave her enough extra to last out the day. When she arrived at the cathedral, she found that the old damp oasis in the shed was frozen solid. With very limited time, and pressing work awaiting at her office, she set about thawing some out, but the only place where she could obtain some hot water quickly was the gentlemen's loo! This turned into a long and laborious job because there are not many slower ways of filling a bucket than using a small wash basin tap. After some time she had sufficient oasis to prepare one vase at the west door which she completed with some foliage she had brought with her. She rushed to her office to see a client, and returned to attempt the second vase, but by then the funeral was nearly due to take place. She hurriedly found a jug in the shed in which she placed the rest of the flowers. It was not at all what she would have liked for such a service, but given the circumstances and the time available it was a fine example of what can be achieved working under extremely difficult conditions, and it illustrates what sort of problems may occur and have to be dealt with solely by the person on the spot.

This event highlighted the problems, and made us consider how we could prevent it recurring. The following year the same two members involved in the above saga got together and produced an excellent selection of greenery including pot-grown ferns and other potted foliage plants. The result was a tremendous improvement on anything that had been done in the past; the plants lasted well, the ferns made excellent growth before Lent, and some have returned for a second season. The main point to consider is that of obtaining different textures and colouring. Some large green decorations can look very dark, and dare one say it – dreary. Laurel in moderation can be an asset, but should be avoided in profusion,

91

and the same applies to several other species.

One year there were two large memorial services which both took place in the nave. Fortunately one relative asked for simple flowers, and the other did not mind what we did, which made everything as easy as it could be. Although flowers can be very expensive at this time of the year, we were able to obtain a good selection wholesale. As it is the Queen Bee's responsibility to telephone the families, in these cases the widows, I find it necessary to adopt a practical approach, although we always try to comply with the wishes of the relatives whenever we can. Advice sometimes has to be given, and of course the cost also must be mentioned. In my experience the relatives are always pleased to be given help with any decisions that arise.

A dried arrangement was included at the High Altar using colours that blended with the altar frontal which was a gift from the Cathedral's Young Friends. It showed up very well from the crossing, and added a most welcome splash of colour at this season. So many dried arrangements in churches tend to be dull, lack

Winter at the High Altar; This display demonstrates that dried flowers can look colourful, it blends well with the altar cloth, and made a welcome addition to the decorations at a difficult time of year.

colour and are left far too long gathering dust. The illustrated example gives some idea of how colourful this type of material can be. It was dismantled on Shrove Tuesday, and some of the pieces will be able to be used for other arrangements when they have been refurbished.

THE HIGH ALTAR

Mechanics Wrought iron stand
Copper urn
Dry oasis

Material *Acanthus spinosus,* Bear's breeches
Artichokes
Hydrangeas
Magnolia grandiflora leaves, Bull bay (US)
Roses, yellow
Solidago x hybrids, Golden rod

Two similar combinations of pot-grown plants and other types of greenery were produced at the screen, and a third major one at the West Door. Some forced pot grown daffodils were included giving a touch of Spring, and this became a genuine Pot-et-Fleur.

THE WEST DOOR

Height overall: 114in (2.95m)
Width: 96in (2.5m) at the widest point

Mechanics Tall wooden pedestal
Large green tub
Oasis
Wire netting

Foliage *Elaeagnus pungens* 'Maculata'
Hedera canariensis 'Variegata', Canary Island ivy
Ilex x altaclarensis 'Golden King', Golden holly
Nephrolepsis exaltata, Ladder fern
Prunus padus, Bird cherry
Taxus baccata, Common yew

Flowers Daffodils, 'Fortune'

Pot-et-Fleur at the West End; Pots of forced daffodils were pushed into the background of different types of foliage, and were easy to remove when the flowers began to fade.

The daffodils did not last long, and I think the hot air from the ducts in the floor caused the problem. All the greenery lasted well. The plants were sprayed as well as being watered which kept them looking both fresh and clean. Do make sure any pot-grown material is given a good soaking before it is included in an arrangement. If it is possible to include peat in a shallow container for pot plants to stand in, it is a good way of making them last a long time with the minimum effort, and it is suitable for a bowl placed on top of a tomb or on some other similar position.

THE NAVE SCREEN – TWO WALL BRACKETS

Height overall: 90in (2.4m)
Width: 60in (1.5m)

Material, Pot-grown	*Ananas comosus* 'Variegatus', Pineapple
	Asplenium nidus, Bird's nest fern
	Dracaena reflexa 'Variegata'
	Fatsia japonica, False castor oil plant
	x *Fatshedera lizei,* Ivy tree, Fatheaded Lizzie
Foliage	*Aucuba japonica,* Spotted laurel
	Choisya ternata, Mexican orange
	Cytisus scoparius, Common broom
	Elaeagnus pungens 'Maculata'
	Hedera canariensis 'Variegata', Canary Island ivy
	Ilex x altaclarensis 'Golden King', Holly
	Ilex aquifolium, Common holly
	Mahonia x 'Charity'
	Phormium tenax, New Zealand flax
	Rhododendron ponticum
	Taxus baccata, Common yew
	Viburnum tinus, Laurustinus

These two large displays of green foliage caused much interest. Whilst working on them a member of the Guild was approached by an admiring visitor who commented, "What lovely flowers. I do like arrangements with all the different greens."
"Thank you." replied the arranger.
"What is that one with the yellow stripe?" asked the visitor.
"Elaeagnus."
"Oh, I never could remember all those names. They sound like horrible skin diseases!"
   I only hope no-one thinks they look like them! It is always nice to receive favourable comments because we certainly aim to give pleasure to as many people

Pot-et-Fleur at the Nave Screen; A magnificent mixture of pot-grown and cut material which provided an excellent range of different shades and textures. It is a good example of a decoration which will last for several weeks without much attention.

as possible, and perhaps some memories to take home with them.

To sum up, now that we have completed a year's work, I hope that you will have found something to interest you which may give you fresh ideas or encourage some of you to attempt big bold constructions for the first time. Recently I spoke to one member who admitted that she had only done flowers on her dining room table before she was involved with the cathedral, but she had obviously learnt a lot, and enjoyed the experience which is really what it is all about.

Tourists from many countries visit Norwich, so Latin, the international botanical language, has been used as much as possible for plant identification. It is well worth learning some of the simple and often repeated adjectives like *variegata*, *multiflora* and *paniculata* because it is rewarding to be able to be certain which plant is being referred to anywhere in the world. The common names often cause some confusion especially when the Americans use different but similar ones to us, consequently where these differ they have been included. Other nations' common names have not been attempted again because the botanical names are universal. Our limit at the cathedral can be summed up by the response to a German visitor who asked *"Was ist das?"* pointing to a bowl of wet oasis. The quick reply of *"Das ist der Blumensteckschaum"* pleased him greatly.

As a parting thought I think the following poem sums up the hard work, but not everyone is ungrateful, I'm pleased to say.

> We, the willing
> Led by the unknowing
> are doing
> The impossible
> for the Ungrateful
>
> We have done so much
> with so little
> for so long
> we are now qualified
> to do anything
> with nothing.

The last twelve months have seen the pile of photographs grow, and it has been a very busy but extremely varied year which has given us a wide choice of events from which to choose. The majority of the arrangements were photographed without giving the decorator any previous warning, and although there has had to be overall planning for the photographic sessions, none were prepared specifically for this book. I have tried to include as many different styles as possible in order that most people will hopefully find something to their liking, but it has not been possible to include everything within the confines of a single volume, much as we would have liked to do so. As I write this, the last photograph has arrived, and our year's record is complete.

The Christmas Spirit; the Vergers placing the Holy Family in position near the screen after moving the tree in the background out of the way.

The Patient Photographer; Robert at work in the nave showing how much equipment was needed to take the majority of illustrations for this book. A far cry from a snapshot!

10

Myths and Legends

I am the Rose of Sharon, and the Lily of the Valleys
The Song of Solomon

egends and symbols have developed over the centuries, and some, adapted from pagan times, are now an accepted part of our Christian worship. The importance of symbolism has regional variations, not only from county to county, but from village to village, and the legends have evolved and changed over the centuries. Some have been lost altogether, and some are as we know them today. It is interesting to discover the deeper meaning behind the use of certain plants at different times of the year, apart from their seasonal availability. For centuries plants and flowers were used for communication throughout the world, and it is from this useage that many of the superstitions and folklore have evolved. Their medicinal qualities were well known to the monks and many country folk, and the language of flowers developed from these beginnings. The examples selected in this chapter have all been associated with decorating places for worship, and because every colour has a distinct meaning, they are listed below:

Black	– Death, sickness
Black & white	– Purity of life
Blue	– The Blessed Virgin Mary, heavenly love
Brown	– Degradation, spiritual death
Gold	– as white
Green	– Spring, hope, charity, life after death
Grey	– Mourning, humility
Purple	– God the Father, royalty
Red	– Love, hate, martyred saints
Violet	– Suffering, truth and love
White	– Purity, innocence of soul
Yellow	– Jealousy, deceit, treason

Floral tributes have been used as offerings to the gods since pagan times, and the practice is continued in India where lotus flowers are offered to Buddha. In China and Japan blossom was placed on altars as early as the T'ang dynasty (618–906 AD).

Early Christians used flowers at funerals to symbolise the Garden of Paradise. Paradise originates from the ancient Persian for an enclosed area, and it was also used in its Hebrew form in the scriptures to describe a similar type of enclosure. (*The Song of Solomon*, Chapter 4, verse 12; *Ecclesiastes*, Chapter 2, verse 5). Two of those most frequently mentioned flowers are roses and lilies, which were placed on the graves of martyrs. Gregory of Tours (538–594 AD) records that garlands were made to hang on walls, but flowers do not appear to have been placed on altars until much later, as the early writers make no mention of the practice. It is interesting that placing flowers upon altars has been losing favour in recent years in this country. The customs that have evolved since the Reformation have been influenced by the church acting as a community centre, not just a place of worship; the nave was cut off from the chancel in order that people could meet without interfering with the sacred part of the building.

Garlands were carried in procession during festivals before they were placed in the church. Professional garland makers were employed, and were no doubt the earliest florists. Records show that roses, laurels, holly and ivy were commonly in use, and were purchased as early as 1483 by city churches. In the country districts, where flowers and foliage were readily available, they would have been supplied by the local people.

Flower gardens intended solely for pleasure were not developed until the 17th century in England. Greenery dominates the early records, and it seems a pity when people object to its use, inferring that it is not worthy of being used to glorify the house of God unless subservient to a lot of blooms. I met one clergyman in a country parish who disliked masses of foliage at Christmas, because he preferred to have flowers for all the decorations. His view may be rather extreme, but everyone has their own personal preferences. Greenery always provides a large and varied selection from which to choose, and it does not have to be drab or uninteresting. I think this point is well illustrated by the photograph of the Pot-et-Fleur in Chapter 9, where the pot grown foliage is used to great advantage. This material is really a continuation of the early use of garlands, and useful suggestions on how to display the different varieties of foliage are contained in Chapter 11.

The use of symbolism was widespread during the Gothic period (1200-1425 AD), and the following list includes a small selection of flowers that would have been available in the late middle ages, and are still in general use today. They were all listed in *The Language of Flowers* by Lady Mary Wortley Montagu (1689-1762), wife of the British ambassador to Constantinople. While in Turkey (1716-18), she adopted their national dress, visited harems, and made a detailed study of their customs and culture.

Angelica	– Inspiration	Holly	– Foresight
Apple blossom	– Preference	Ivy	– Fidelity, marriage
Balsam	– Consolation	Laurel	– Glory
Borage	– Courage	Lilac	– White – youthful
Broom	– Neatness		innocence
Cedar	– Strength	Lily	– White – fidelity,
Chrysanthemums	– Red – I love		purity
	– White – truth	Michaelmas Daisy	– Afterthought
	– Yellow – slighted	Oak	– Strength
	love	Privet	– Prohibition
Columbine	– The Virgin's rose	Rose	– Divine Love, the
Crown Imperial	– Majesty, power		Blessed Virgin Mary
Daffodil	– Regard		– Red – Flower of
Dahlia	– Instability		martyrs
Fruit	– Achievement		– Symbol of silence
Apple	– Man's fall	Rosemary	– Remembrance

Gladioli	– Ready armed	Stock	– Lasting beauty
Golden Rod	– Precaution	Sweet Bay	– Wisdom
Grain	– Bread of the Sacrament	Tulip	– Fame
Grapevine	– Christ and Disciples		

Wheatears were originally a symbol of fertility to the Romans and have been carved on furniture and architecture throughout the ages, but they are now used only for Harvest Thanksgiving. Gladioli also symbolically represent the Incarnation of Christ, abundance and generosity.

Nearly every flower has a meaning, and in the 19th century they became a popular form of romantic communication. The flower language as such originated in Moslem countries where the harem occupants used flowers to communicate, often anonymously and in secret. The origins go back many centuries, and there are records of symbolic finds in the tomb of Tutankhamun. Columbines, from their likeness to doves, were used in the middle ages as symbols of the Holy Spirit, and they were depicted in Renaissance art. Rosemary was believed to improve memory, which no doubt explains Ophelia's 'There's rosemary, that's for remembrance; pray you love, remember.' (*Hamlet,* Act IV, scene V).

Rose petals were frequently used at weddings by the Romans, rose being an anagram of Eros, the god of love. At important festivals rosemary and fennel would be included with other sweet smelling herbs. Houses and other buildings were decorated, and aromatic plants including many evergreen herbs were used to improve the general aroma. Tussie-mussies or nosegays were carried to ward off the unpleasant smells encountered in everyday living.

There has been a tremendous renewal of interest in pot-pourri, and this is another traditional way to use aromatic herbs and flowers. From such beginnings, many of the sweetly scented flowers have become symbols of Christian belief, and are used in the Church's daily worship.

Lilies of the valley are among the first flowers to bloom, are associated with the announcement of Spring, and have become the symbol of the Advent of Christ. The pure whiteness of its petals and its sweet scent made it a symbol of the Virgin Mary, and especially of her immaculate conception; the latter being based on *The Song of Solomon* 'I am the rose of Sharon, and the lily of the valleys.' Our Lady's tears and the Ladder to heaven are two of the names by which they are known and, according to legend, it always grows where a saint has died. The leaves contain a green dye, and it also has medicinal properties as a cardiac stimulant, sometimes being used when *Digitalis* fails. The common foxglove is a well known stimulant, and has several names including Gloves of Our Lady and Dead men's bells.

Laurus nobilis, the sweet bay or the true laurel of Greece and Rome, was used as crowns for heroes, victors and poets because the leaves reflected light, and it has since become the symbol of wisdom. It contains an antiseptic oil, the sweetly scented wood is used in marquetry, and some Americans use it as a caterpillar repellent. Lilac and hawthorn are both pollinated by insects, and no doubt this has given rise to the superstition that it is unlucky to bring them inside. *Crataegus monogyna,* the common hawthorn, is avoided by both bees and butterflies, because of the faint odour resembling decaying fish caused by the plant containing a mixture of coumarin and aminoid compound. Legends warn that these flowers depict impending death, although the Romans used it as a symbol of marriage.

Crataegus monogyna 'Biflora', the Glastonbury thorn, takes its name from St Joseph of Arimathea's arrival in England to found Christianity during the 1st century. He visited Glastonbury and, disappointed by his lack of success, thrust his staff into the ground and prayed for a miracle. The staff burst into leaf and flowered on what was Christmas day until the calendar change in 1751. This plant should not be confused with the true thorn of the crown of thorns, *Paliurus spina-christi* or Christ's thorn, which is a native of Southern Europe and West Asia that will also grow in the British Isles.

Archangelica officinalis, angelica, has been a symbol of the Holy Trinity since the 9th century, and has been called the herb of the Holy Ghost. It was used in decorations, became known as angelica for its angelical virtues, and also has medicinal value.

The red *Rosa gallica* is the Christian symbol of martyrdom, and the white *R. allium* represents purity. The feast of Corpus Christi was celebrated with garlands of red roses.

Lilium candidum, the Madonna flower, has become associated with paintings of the Virgin and Child, and has been cultivated for over 3,000 years. In the 13th century the scholar Bartholomaeus Anglicus described it thus: 'The Lily is a herb with white flowers and though the leaves of the flowers be white, yet within shineth the likeness of gold.' The lily's story has been ascribed with historical and religious significance. There are several varieties to which this applies, and *Fritillaria imperialis* or the Crown Imperial, which is often in bloom at Easter, has a legend associated with it that makes its inclusion in the Easter decorations most appropriate. The legend tells how the flowers that form the lily's head once all looked towards the sky rather than hanging down as they do now. In the garden of Gethsemane where Jesus walked and prayed, the flowers and lilies were fond of him, because he was gentle and never trod on them or broke their stems. When they heard that Jesus was to die, they decided to bow their heads in sympathy. However, the haughty Crown Imperial refused to bow. When Jesus passed by, this proud flower alone held its head upright, while the rest bent down. Jesus stopped, looked sadly at the lily, and then walked on. The lily was so ashamed that it hung its head at last, and wept. If you look inside the bells of the Crown Imperial you can still see the tears for ever marking its shame, and it has never held its head up again.

Ilex aquifolium, Holly or Holy holly, was one of the first trees to be used in early decorating; it was a symbol of peace and goodwill in Roman times, and was even used as a lightning conductor. The elder Pliny (23-79 AD) commented on its branches' ability to defend houses in his *Naturalis Historia.* It was also thought to protect men from witchcraft. Holly is known to have been used since 500 BC at Midwinter pagan festivals, and later in *The Language of Flowers* represented foresight. It also possesses medicinal properties, but church records of the 1850s show that sextons used it as a symbol of peace at Christmas. A good decorative variety is *Ilex x Altaclarensis* 'Lawsoniana' which has vivid yellow variegations, and should be grown in full sunlight in fertile soil. The semi-spineless evergreen leaves appear very similar to *Eleagnus pungens* 'Maculata'.

Saint-foin or Sainfoin, *Onobrychis viciifolia*, has a charming legend associated with it, which is particularly suitable for children at Christmas. It is said that some Saint-Foin herbs lay amongst the hay in the stable at Bethlehem, and they became most interested in the Baby. When the shepherds arrived to worship the Infant, they too wanted to honour Him, and when darkness came the pink flowers twisted around until they formed a crown around the Baby's head. The name Saint-foin, Norman French for Holy or Sacred hay, has been used since that day.

Other plants which are used occasionally in various decorations also have interesting stories attached to them. *Molucella*, although sometimes referred to as the Bells of Ireland has no connection with that country at all, and its true name, shell flower, is derived from its shell-like calyx which surrounds and dominates the small white flowers. The long sprays of apple green 'flowers' or calces are attractively netted, and may be used either dry, when they become a pretty parchment colour, or freshly cut.

Borago officinalis, borage, is deep blue, the colour of Christ, and the flower's five-pointed crown symbolises the five wounds of the crucified Christ. The five stamens are bent towards each other, and appear at first glance to be only three. Borage was therefore also depicted representing the Holy Trinity. Its medicinal properties were used to treat a number of complaints, but the dried herb was never utilised.

Malva althaea officinalis, mallow, has well known medicinal properties, the healing power of its leaves was recorded by Pythagoras, and its name derives from the Greek *altheo* – I heal. Mallow in paintings symbolises the prayer of forgiveness and pardon.

In Mexico, *Euphorbia pulcherrima*, the poinsettia, is known as the Nativity flower from its association with a charming legend. It recounts how, one Christmas Eve, a poor orphan girl walked towards the cathedral to pray to the Blessed Virgin Mary, when she noticed that everyone except herself had a gift to offer. She stopped and picked a white poinsettia growing by the wayside. When the girl entered the cathedral, she placed the flower on the altar where it turned from white to scarlet. Since then it has always been known as the Nativity flower.

Finally, I include *Passiflora middletoniana*, the Passion flower, because it can be most effective when hung down a pedestal to form part of the petticoats. It symbolises the Passion of our Lord. The ten petals composing the perianth represent the Apostles, excluding Peter for his denial and Judas for betraying Christ. The flower's filaments are the nimbus or glory, the stalked ovary resembles a hammer, and the three styles with rounded heads are the nails. It is completed by the five stamens representing the five wounds of Christ.

I am sure many of you will know other legends. I have not attempted to provide a complete list, but I hope that this will encourage you to discover more, especially ones which may be unique to your locality, and perhaps incorporate them in some of your arrangements at an appropriate time.

11

A Selection of Foliage for all Seasons

n this chapter I will give you some idea of the variety of foilage regularly used in the cathedral, and although the accompanying list does not set out to be comprehensive, it does include all the material we have found to be both reliable and effective. For easy reference the greenery has been divided into groups according to their colours.

Preparation is the key to keeping foliage looking fresh, and is just as important as conditioning for the flowers. Nearly all types appreciate a long thorough soak the night before being used, and the lives of most flowers can be extended considerably by treating their foliage carefully. There are some whose blooms will last almost twice as long if stripped of their leaves. Sometimes the original greenery can be used with the flowers, but not attached to the same stem, although the effect is unchanged. In the Spring, the first greenery available includes the lovely fresh green of young beech leaves and attractive long drooping larch stems. If you have these in an arrangement, there really is no need to add anything else, and their preparation only requires trimming the stalks and giving them a good soak.

Young maple and oak can look extremely pretty, but do not last well unless the leaf buds are sufficiently open. The same applies to immature whitebeam which will turn very dark at the edges if cut too soon, and in my view is not suitable for forcing. The different varieties of poplars must also be used with caution, because they too blacken easily. The leaves of daffodils and arum lilies enhance their respective flowers, but both are soft and tend to go soggy in water if immersed for too long.

As Spring turns into Summer there is an abundant variety of both soft and woody foliage, and also a good choice of colours including silver and gold, dark and light green and many variegated forms. Perhaps the most often used is *Ligustrum ovalifolium* 'Aureum', golden privet, but again do wait until it is properly in leaf before cutting.

Hostas are among the best of the soft material, and there is enough variety to suit every need. Their leaves range from blue to grey and some have bright variegated foliage. The flowers are generally insignificant, but some are scented.

Grey foliage is always popular and useful for many different purposes. There are many suitable plants but, because they are mostly soft stemmed, it is advisable to make sure the stems are clear of leaves when in water otherwise they turn soggy and smelly. *Senecio leucostachys* is one of the best silver leaved semi-shrubby plants, and as it originally came from the semi-desert in Patagonia it is used to cold frosty nights. It will withstand being dry and starved, but does not like very wet conditions so should be protected from the rain. The big cardoon leaves are spectacular in a large building, and are a joy at weddings if you can obtain them at the right time. However it is essential to prepare them properly using the boiling water treatment.

The lime bursts into flower in about Midsummer, and there is nothing more delicate than its stripped branches showing either the buds or the seed pods later in the season. Do be careful of bees when you pick lime as they adore its scent and will fly miles to work the insignificant but sweet smelling flowers.

This is an appropriate place to mention the multitude of ferns which all need careful preparation. (A flower which always springs to mind alongside ferns is *Digitalis* or the common foxglove and its up-market relatives the *Digitalis excelsior* hybrids whose leaves are good but soft. They mix excellently with ferns as one acts as a natural foil for the other, woodlands being the natural habitat of both.) *Adiantum*, the maidenhair ferns, are ideal for weddings, and the almost evergreen *Asplenium*, spleenwort, is attractive and shiny with long narrow fronds. There are several deciduous *Dryopteris*, Buckler ferns, which mix well with other foliage and flowers. *D. filix-mas*, the male fern, is perhaps the most common variety. It is robust, grows well, and although unsuitable in a small garden is excellent if room can be found to accomodate it.

When Autumn arrives the changing leaf patterns provide a limitless variety of colours from which to choose, but do take care because some will not last long, and it is wiser to gather them before the colours turn too much. Some of the autumnal foliage can be preserved for later in the year, but the expense of preparing sufficient branches for use in the larger arrangements by the glycerin method should be considered. My own view is that there is enough fresh material available throughout the year to make this additional cost unnecessary.

Golden privet, cardoons and hostas are all still available in the Autumn. Foliage with berries is a bonus, but care has to be taken to avoid having squashed berries underfoot, as many cause very bad stains. The many varieties of cotoneaster, which go so well with chrysanthemums, last well, and their berries remain in place. The *Euonymous europaeus* and *E. fortunei* 'Silver Queen' spindles, both natives of Europe, have pretty pink lobes which open to display their bright orange seeds, and can be used with most autumnal flowers. The wood is very hard which is why it was chosen to make the spindles for spinning wheels, hence the name.

The arrival of Winter brings the decorator's high spot of Christmas. Holly is immediately evocative of the season, but it can look dark and dreary unless it is well berried and placed in the light. The silver and gold variegated hollies are preferable for large arrangements as they show up so well, again always providing they are sufficiently well lit. I like to use variegated conifers whenever I need this sort of material, and *Thuya plicata* 'Aureovariegata', the Western red cedar, is a firm favourite as it will last for weeks if it is just kept damp. Common yew and its other forms are also available. *Prunus laurocerasus*, known as English laurel in America, can be used in either its green or variegated form as well as many species of ivy and preserved beech leaves.

At all times of the year there are so many varieties of evergreen box readily available that it is worthwhile looking for some of the less common ones. It is possible to find these hardy trees and shrubs with golden tipped or blue grey foliage and a very fine drooping variety. *Buxus sempervirens* 'Elegantissima', variegated box, with its glossy oval shaped leaves outlined with a creamy yellow margin is well worth having. All these shrubs have their uses, and I would not be without any of them, especially as they will even last for a considerable time out of water. In fact they usually get dusty before they die!

The different types of ivy are enjoying increasing popularity after a period of decline, which was no doubt a reaction against Victorian and Edwardian fashion. In those days the nursery catalogues always included a large selection of varieties. Today one of the best decorative variegated ivies has to be *Hedera colchica dentata* 'Variegata'. Some will grow as free standing bushes, others as ground cover or they can provide excellent camouflage for steps, drain covers, old tree stumps and other objects which are better disguised. *Hedera helix* is a smaller variety but similar to *H. colchica*. *Hedera helix* 'Cavendishii' is a very old variegated ivy, which will withstand frost, and was even mentionned by the elder Pliny (AD 23-79) in his *Naturalis Historia*. Some of these ivies such as *Hedera helix* 'Glacier' make good house plants, but it is not as hardy as the 'Cavendishii', and grows slowly. *Hedera canariensis*, another house plant, will grow outside but is a little too tender for a hard winter. There are thousands of different ivies, and as over 3,000 have been listed, I am sure you can find some to suit your requirements. They can be used in a large arrangement as long drooping petticoats, for decorating the Advent ring, or as part of the Pot-et-Fleur illustrated in Chapter 9. If possible do try some different varieties.

The several good varieties of dogwoods have coloured stems as an added attraction, making them particularly useful in the Spring. Next, *Elaeagnus pungens* 'Maculata' is a superb, long lasting, golden variegated bush, and *E. x ebbingei* 'Gilt Edge' is a hardy shrub with bright yellow and green leaves which are sometimes almost totally yellow. *Euonymus radicans* 'Variegatus',which both trails and climbs, is well worth using, and keeps its bright yellow bias throughout the entire Winter.

There is a wide range of laurels available, and all have their uses for decorating. The *Aucuba japonica*, spotted laurel, is preferable to the rather dark and heavy plain variety, although the latter can be invaluable on occasions, and its small white flowers are very useful in the Spring. *Prunus lusitanicia*, Portugal laurel, has dark green glossy leaves throughout the year which make an excellent background for most other foliage and flowers. We must not forget *Laurus nobilis* or bay laurel, the true laurel of the ancients, whose fragrant leaves can be an added attraction in some places. Do not despise laurels because they all have their uses and most are available thoughout the year. *Garrya elliptica* is a must for its greyish green cascading tassels full of yellow pollen which mix so well with other material, especially early daffodils.

Next I have a few suggestions for a choice of material for using in the large decorations suitable for weddings and similar occasions. The foliage really will make all the difference, and can turn a normal sized arrangement into a big, bold striking display that will help to make the occasion memorable for everyone attending. One of the best, now that it is more readily available, is *Acanthus spinosus*, bear's breeches, which has dramatic spikes on its deeply incised leaves. *Atriplex hortensis* 'Rubra' can be grown easily from seed, and it too has a dramatic quality especially when it has seed heads; sparrows are said to like the leaves. *Atriplex halimus*, Tree Purslane, originally from southern Europe, is a medium semi-evergreen shrub with silvery grey leaves. *Phormium tenax* has leaf blades the length of a sword, and the smaller *P.colensoi* can be used to give a sharp line to an arrangement. The greyish green *P.tenax*, New Zealand flax or hemp in America, will grow to a height of about 6ft (2m).

Ornamental rhubarb can be used with large substantial material because the leaves are suitable for disguising a container by hanging over the sides, and *Rheum palmatum* 'Atrosanguineum' has a pleasant red colour on the underside of its leaves. Another plant suitable for the same purpose is *Rodgersia tabularis* whose leaves are lime green in colour. One more in this group must be *Cynara cardunculus*, the cardoon, whose seed heads although decorative are also extremely heavy. Care must be taken to secure them in a stable position in case they collapse taking everything else with them!

The huge leaves of *Fatsia japonica* look like overgrown fig leaves averaging 1ft (30cm) across with a lovely glossy appearance which can add another dimension to any decoration. *Mahonia lomarifolia* has leaves over 1½ft (50cm) long, but this variety is not completely hardy. I make no excuse for ending this list with the versatile *Ligustrum ovalifolium* 'Aureum', golden privet, because I have used it in lengths of upto 8ft (2.5m), and it has never looked too heavy. Some people think of privet as being boring, but its rate of growth must be a consideration as it replenishes itself so quickly; in fact the more it is cut the better it grows. So, when cost is an important factor, it has to be a good choice with the added benefit that it is easy to grow providing it receives enough sunlight to keep its bright colouring.

This chapter has been restricted to selecting the most well tried manageable material. The subject warrants a book entirely of its own, and it would be pointless to try and give a comprehensive list in the available space, nor will I take up a lot of this chapter giving details of all the flowering shrubs and plants renowned for their berries. Do please look at the following list and try some of the suggestions yourself.

GREENERY FOR ALL OCCASIONS

Conditioning – All hardwood foliage requires the bark stripped for about 2in (50cm) from the cut end, the wood split, and then a long soak, preferably over night, before it is used. The letters following each entry refer to the various methods of preparatory conditioning, and are listed in the following chapter's notes on flowers.

Synonyms – Where a tree or plant's botannical name has been changed, the correct name has been listed first, and the older name, by which many plants are still widely known, is given as a synonym.

COPPER AND PURPLE

Acer platanoides,	Norway maple, several varieties	A D
Atriplex hortensis 'Rubra'	Orach	D
Berberis vulgaris 'Atropurpurea'	Purple-leaf barberry	D
Corylus maxima 'Purpurea'	Purple-leaf filbert (US)	A D
Cotinus coggyria 'Foliis Purpureis', syn. *Rhus cotinus*	Smoke tree (US)	B
Fagus sylvatica 'Riversii'	Purple beech	D
Phormium tenax 'Purpureum'	New Zealand flax	E
Prunus cerasifera 'Pissardii'	Myrobalan, Purple-leaf plum	A D
Rosa rubrifolia		A D
Weigela florida 'Foliis Purpureis'	Purple-leaf weigela	A

SILVER AND VARIEGATED

Acer negundo 'Variegatum'	Box elder	A D
Artemesia absinthium 'Lambrook Silver'	Wormwood, Absinth	A
Cynara cardunculus	Cardoon, Artichoke	B
Cornus controversa 'Variegata'	Japanese dogwood	A D
Cornus florida 'Tricolor'	Flowering dogwood	A D
Cornus mas	Cornelian cherry (US)	A D
Cornus alba 'Elegantissima'	Dogwood	A D
Elaeagnus x ebbingei		A D
Eucalyptus gunnii	Cider gum (US)	A D
Eucalyptus globulus	Tasmanian blue gum (US)	A D
Eucalyptus perriniana	Round-leaf snow gum, Spinning gum	A D
Garrya elliptica		A D
Ilex aquifolium 'Silver Queen'	Common holly	A D
Phormium tenax 'Variegatum'	New Zealand flax	E
Pyrus salicifolia	Willow leaf pear (US)	A D

Senecio maritima, syn. *Cineraria maritima*	Sea ragwort	A
Senecio leucostachys		A
Sorbus aria	Common whitebeam (US)	A D
Weigela praecox 'Variegata'	Variegated weigela	A D

GOLD AND VARIEGATED

Acer negundo 'Auretum'	Box elder, Ash-leaved maple	A D
Aucuba japonica 'Goldenheart'	Gold-dust tree (US), Japanese laurel, Spotted laurel	A D
Buxus sempervirens 'Gold Tip'	Common box	A D
Elaeagnus pungens 'Maculata'		A D
Euonymus fortunei, syn. *E. radicans* 'Silver Queen'	Spindle tree	B
Hedera canariensis 'Variegata', syn. 'Gloire de Marengo'	Madeira ivy (US)	A
Hedera helix 'Silver Queen', syn. 'Marginata'	Common ivy	A
Ilex x altaclarensis 'Golden King'	Highclere holly	A D
Ligustrum ovalifolium 'Aureum'	Golden privet	A D
Ligustrum lucidum 'Tricolor'	Privet	A D
Sambucus racemosa 'Plumosa Aurea'	Red berried elder	A D

GREEN

Acer platanoides	Norway maple	A D
Aspidistra elatior	Parlour palm, Cast-iron plant	E
Bergenia leaves	Pig squeak	E
Buxus sempervirens	Common box	A
Fagus sylvatica	Common beech	A
Fatsia japonica leaves, syn. *Aralia japonica*	False castor oil plant, Japan Fatsia (US)	E
x *Fatshedera lizei*	Fatshedera, Aralia ivy (US)	E
Hosta sieboldiana leaves, syn. *Funkia*	Hosta (US)	A
Hosta plantaginea	Day lily, Plantain lily (US)	A
Laurus nobilis	Bay laurel, Sweet bay, Bay (US)	D
Molucella laevis	Bells of Ireland (US)	G H
Phormium tenax	New Zealand flax	E
Phormium colensoi	Mountain flax	E
Pittosporum tenuifolium, syn. *P.nigricans*		D E

Polygonatum multiflorum	Solomon's seal, David's harp	E
Prunus lusitanica	Portugal laurel	D
Prunus laurocerasus	Common laurel, Cherry laurel (US)	B
Quercus species	Oak (young foliage)	D
Salix caprea	Pussy or Goat willow, Great sallow	D
Stephanandra incisa, syn. *S. flexuosa*		D
Tilia x europaea, syn. *T. vulgaris*	Common lime, Linden tree	D G
Viburnum tinus	Laurustinus, Laurestinus (US)	D
Viburnum opulus 'Sterile'	British guelder rose, Snowball bush, European cranberry bush (US)	D G

CONIFERS

Abies procera, syn. *A. nobilis*	Noble fir (US)	A
Chamaecyparis pisifera 'Plumosa'	Sawara cypress	A
Chamaecyparis pisifera 'Squarrosa'	Sawara cypress	A
x Cupressocyparis leylandii	Leyland cypress	A
Juniperus communis	Common juniper	A
Larix europaea	European larch	A
Mahonia x 'Charity'	Mahonia	A
Picea abies, syn. *P. excelsa*	Common spruce, Norway spruce	A
Thuja plicata 'Aureovariegata', syn. *T. lobbii* 'Zebrina'	Western red cedar, Giant arborvitae (US)	A
Taxus baccata	Common yew, English yew (US)	A
Taxus baccata 'Aurea'	Golden yew	A

FERNS

Adiantum capillus-veneris	Maidenhair fern, Venus-hair (US)	C
Asparagus plumosus	Asparagus fern	C
Asplenium	Spleenwort	C
Asplenium scolopendrium	Hart's tongue fern	C
Dryopteris linnaeana	Oak fern, St Christophe herb	C
Dryopteris austriaca	Buckler fern	C
Osmunda regalis	Royal fern, Flowering fern	C
Polystichum falcatum, syn. *Cyrtomium falcatum*	Japanese holly fern (US)	C

12

Flowers for All Seasons, in All Colours

Seasons – Although the flowers are grouped under each season by colour, the months when they are usually in bloom are shown alongside the botannical and common names, for example 2-5 denotes February to May. Fl. refers to a plant normally available from florists throughout the year.
Height – The average height is given except where the entry refers to a climber, bush or tree.
Conditioning – Code letters, listed in the following text, refer to the different methods of conditioning each flower requires.

WHITE AND CREAM
Spring

Narcissus, species Daffodils	2-5	1-1½ft	(30-45cm)	A
Prunus avium, Common flowering cherry	–	tree/shrub		D
Syringa vulgaris, Common lilac	4-5	tree/shrub		G
Tulip hybrids	2-5	1-2ft	(30-60cm)	A
Zantedeschia aethiopica, Arum or Pig lily	4-6	2-3ft	(60-90cm)	A

Summer

Achillea ptarmica 'The Pearl', Sneezewort (US)	7-9	2-2½ft	(90-125cm)	A
Agapanthus africanus, syn. *A. umbellatus*, African agapanthus, Lily-of-the-Nile (US)	6-8	2-3ft	(60-90cm)	A
Campanula pyramidalis, Steeple or Chimney bellflower	7-8	3-5ft	(90-150cm)	F
Chrysanthemum maximum 'Wirral Pride', Shasta daisy	7-9	3ft	(90cm)	A
Clematis montana 'Alba', Mountain clematis	–	climber		A B
Delphinium elatum hybrids	6-7	3-5ft	(90-125cm)	F
Dianthus, Perpetual flowering carnations	Fl.	2-3ft	(60-90cm)	A I
Digitalis purpurea 'Excelsior' hybrids, Foxgloves	5-6	5ft	(1.5m)	F
Gladioli hybrids, Sword lily, Corn flag	6-8	2-3ft	(60-90cm)	A
Gypsophila paniculata, Baby's breath, Chalk plant	6-8	1-2ft	(30-60cm)	A I
Hosta sieboldiana, syn. *Funkia*, Hosta (US)	5-6	1ft	(30cm)	A
Hydrangea paniculata	6-7	shrub		B E J
Iris hybrids, Dutch iris	5-6	1-2ft	(30-60cm)	A
Lathyrus odoratus, Sweet pea	1-6	1-1½ft	(30-45cm)	A
Lavatera trimestris, syn. *L. rosea*, Mallow	6-8	3-4ft	(90-125cm)	B D
Lilium candidum, Madonna lily (US)	6-7	4-6ft	(1.25-2m)	A
Lilium longiflorium, Easter lily (US)	7-8	2½-3ft	(80-100cm)	A
Lupinus polyphyllus, Lupin	6-8	2-4ft	(60-125cm)	G
Matthiola incana, Stock, various	6-8	1-1½ft	(30-45cm)	A
Nicotiana affinis, Tobacco plant	6-8	2-3ft	(60-90cm)	A
Paeonia officinalis, Common paeony	5-6	2-3ft	(60-90cm)	A
Phlox paniculata, syn. *P. decussata*	7-10	2-3½ft	(60-100cm)	A
Rose hybrids, florist's and outdoor	6-9			A K

Autumn

Aster novi-belgii, Michaelmas daisy, Starwort	9-10	2-3ft	(60-90cm)	A
Chrysanthemums, outdoor	8-10	2-3ft	(60-90cm)	B D
Spray				
Spider				
Single				
Double				
Pom-pom				
Throughout the year from florists				
Dahlias, many different varieties including decorative and cactus	7-10	1-3ft	(30-90cm)	A

GREEN

Alchemilla mollis, Lady's mantle	5-6	1-1½ft	(30-45cm)	A
Amaranthus candatus, Love-lies-bleeding (US)	8-9	2ft	(60cm)	G
Angelica archangelica, Garden angelica (US)	6-8	2-4ft	(60-125cm)	F
Chrysanthemums, all the year	Fl.	2-3ft	(60-90cm)	B D
Eucomis punctata, Pineapple lily, Rings flower	5-6	2ft	(60cm)	A
Euphorbia characias, Spurge, Milkweed	6-11	4ft	(1.25m)	B
Euphorbia wulfenii, syn. *E. venata*, Spurge	6-11	4ft	(1.25m)	B
Molucella laevis, Bells of Ireland	6-	2ft	(60cm)	G H

YELLOW AND GOLD
Spring

Cytisus scoparius, Common broom, Scotch broom (US)	3-5	shrub		D
Forsythia x intermedia, Golden-bell tree (US)	12-3	shrub		D
Fritillaria imperialis, Crown imperial	4-6	3ft	(90cm)	A
Iris hybrids, Dutch iris	5-6	1-2ft	(30-60cm)	B
Narcissus, species Daffodils	2-5	1-1½ft	(3-45cm)	A
Tulip hybrids	2-5	1-2ft	(30-60cm)	A

Summer

Aconitum lycoctonum, Monkshood, Wolfsbane (US)	7-8	3ft	(90cm)	D
Eremurus robustus, Foxtail lily, King's spear (US)	6-7	3ft	(90cm)	D
Gladioli hybrids, Sword lily, Corn flag	6-8	2-3ft	(60-90cm)	D
Hypericum calycinum, Rose of Sharon, St John's Wort (US)	7-8	8-24in	(20-60cm)	D
Kniphofia, Red hot poker, Torch lily	6-8	2-3ft	(60-90cm)	A
Lupinus arboreus, Tree lupin	6-8	2-4ft	(60-125cm)	G
Lupinus polyphillus, Lupin	6-8	2-4ft	(60-125cm)	G
Rudbeckia hirta, Black-eyed Susan	7-9	2-2½ft	(60-75cm)	B

Autumn

Achillea filipendulina 'Gold Plate', Noble yarrow	7-10	2½-4ft	(75-125cm)	A
Alstromeria aurantica, Peruvian lily, Lily of the Incas (US)	Fl.	1½-2½ft	(45-75cm)	A
Chrysanthemums – see white				B D
Dahlias – see white				A
Roses – see white				A K
Solidago x hybrida, Golden rod	9-10	5ft	(1.5m)	D

RED

Spring

Tulip hybrids	2-5	1-2ft	(30-60cm)	A

Summer

Alstromeria ligtu hybrids, Peruvian lily, Lily of the Incas (US)	Fl.	1½-2½ft	(45-75cm)	A
Callistephus chinensis, China aster (US)	7-9	9-15in	(23-38cm)	D
Chrysanthemums – florist's – see white				B D
Dianthus, species Carnations – see white				E I
Euphorbia griffithii 'Fireglow', Spurge	6-11	4ft	(1.25m)	B
Gladioli – see white				D
Kniphofia, Red hot poker, Torch lily	6-8	2-3ft	(60-90cm)	A E
Lathyrus odoratus, Sweet pea	5-6	1-1½ft	(30-45cm)	B E
Lupinus polyphyllus, Lupin	6-8	2-4ft	(60-125cm)	G
Paeonia officinalis, Common paeony	5-6	2-3ft	(60-90cm)	B G
Pyrethrum roseum, syn. *Chrysanthemum coccineum*, Painted daisy	6-8	1½-2ft	(45-60cm)	B
Rose hybrids – see white				A K

Autumn

Amaranthus caudatus, Love-lies-bleeding (US)	8-9	2ft	(60cm)	A G
Amaranthus tricolor, Joseph's coat (US)	8-9	2ft	(60cm)	A G
Chrysanthemums – see white				B D
Dahlias – see white				A
Euphorbia pulcherrima, Poinsettia	11-	shrub		B
Phlox paniculata, syn. *P. decussata*	7-10	2-3½ft	(60-100cm)	D

PINK

Spring

Blossoms: *Prunus*, *Malus*, etc				D
Lathyrus odoratus, Sweet pea	5-6	1-1½ft	(30-45cm)	B E

Summer

Carnations	Fl.			E I

Clematis montana, Clematis		climber	B
Delphinium consolida, Larkspur	6-7	3ft (90cm)	F
Hydrangea macrophylla, syn. *H.hortensis*, Common hydrangea, House hydrangea (US)	6-7	shrub	B E J
Lathyrus odoratus, Sweet pea	5-6	1-1½ft (30-45cm)	B F
Matthiola incana, Stock	6-8	1-1½ft (30-45cm)	A
Paeonia officinalis, Common garden paeony	5-6	2-3ft (60-90cm)	B
Phlox paniculata, syn. *P. decussata*	7-10	2-3½ft (60-100cm)	D
Pyrethrum roseum, syn. *Chrysanthemum coccineum*	6-8	1½-2ft (45-60cm)	B
Rose hybrids, floribundas and older varieties			A K
Syringa vulgaris, Common lilac	4-5	shrub	B D G
Weigela florida, syn. *Diervilla florida*, Bush honeysuckle, Weigela	5-6	shrub	D

Autumn

Alstromeria ligtu hybrids, Peruvian lily, Lily of the Incas (US)	Fl.	1½-2½ft (45-75cm)	A
Chrysanthemums – see white			B D
Dianthus, Perpetual flowering carnations	Fl.	2-3ft (60-90cm)	A I
Gladioli hybrids, Sword lily, Corn flag	6-8	2-3ft (60-90cm)	A
Nerine sarniensis, Guernsey lily	9-11	1½-2ft (45-60cm)	B
Phlox paniculata, syn. *P. decussata*	7-10	2-3½ft (60-100cm)	D

BLUE, LILAC AND MAUVE
Spring

Iris hybrids, Dutch iris	5-6	1-2ft (30-60cm)	B
Syringa vulgaris, Common lilac	4-5	shrub	B D G

Summer

Aconitum lycoctonum, Wolfsbane (US)	7-8	3ft (90cm)	D
Aconitum napellus, Monkshood	5-6	3-4ft (90-125cm)	D
Agapanthus africanus, syn. *A. umbellatus*, African agapanthus, Lily-of-the-Nile (US)	6-8	2-3ft (60-90cm)	A
Campanula medium, Canterbury Bell	7-8	3-5ft (90-150cm)	B
Campanula pyramidalis, Steeple or Chimney bellflower	7-8	3-5ft (90-150cm)	B
Cynara cardunculus, Cardoon	7-10	3-5ft (90-150cm)	B
Delphinium consolida, Larkspur	6-7	3ft (90cm)	F
Delphinium hybrids, large flowered	6-7	3-5ft (90-150cm)	G
Hydrangea macrophylla, syn. *H. hortensis*, Common hydrangea, House hydrangea (US)	6-8	shrub	B E J
Iris, English	6-7	1-2ft (30-60cm)	A
Lathyrus odoratus, Sweet pea	5-6	1-1½ft (30-45cm)	B F
Lupinus polyphillus, Lupin	6-8	2-4ft (60-125cm)	F

Matthiola incana, Stock	6-8	1-2ft	(30-60cm)	A
Scabiosa caucasica, Scabious, Pincushion flower	6-7	1½-2ft	(45-60cm)	A

A FEW PASTEL SHADES

Freesias	Fl.	9-15in	(23-38cm)	A
Gerbera jamesonii, Transvaal, Barbertown (US)	Fl.	9-15in	(23-38cm)	A

WHITE AND PURPLE

Acanthus spinosus, Bear's breeches, Artist's acanthus (US)	6-8	3-4ft	(90-125cm)	B

CONDITIONING

Three points should be remembered when using blooms purchased from a florist:

a. Recut the stems with a sharp knife after purchase.

b. Clean your containers because bacteria will close the cut stems.

c. Recut stems and change water to prolong their life.

The main methods of conditioning which apply to both flowers and foliage are:

A. All flowers and shrubs need the stems trimming, the bottom leaves removing, and a long soak in water before use.

B. Place the stems in boiling water to seal them, then immediately plunge into cold water. Some plants, like members of the *Euphorbia,* spurge, family, exude poison so try not to get it on your skin, because it can cause a rash.

C. Burn the ends of the stems with a lighter, candle or match to seal them.

D. Cut, split or crush the ends of the stems to improve the water flow.

E. Some foliage is better if soaked overnight, immersed in a tub of cold water.

F. Hollow stems can be filled with water then pluggd with cotton wool to make them last longer.

G. It is necessary to defoliate the branches of some shrubs to prolong the life of the blooms.

H. Some plants will benefit from being plunged straight into water providing you can take a bucket with you whilst picking, but most will survive for a short time out of water.

I. Cut all dianthus species (carnations) between the nodules (joints)

J. Hydrangeas do not like oasis, possibly because it blocks the flow of water to these very thirsty plants. Do try placing them in plain water.

K. Roses, dethorn the stems.

In order to keep the stems of tulips straight before use, they can be wrapped in newspaper and then put in water. All flowers like adequate ventilaton and clean water. They do not like damp conditions or being too hot or dry as when placed on the grills over central heating pipes. Certain plants and blooms require a specific amount of light, for example poinsettias prefer a west window. You will find that cut flowers will last longer in a place where the direct rays of the sun do not reach them for long periods. If you can add a foxglove the effect of the digitalis will make the arrangement last longer. There are several other ways of extending the life of many of the different cut flowers and foliage we use. Copper coins placed in the water with roses is one such example, but as there are so many I have not included all the uses of water additives or the other ways which are only suitable for one or two odd varieties. The above methods are adequate for the majority of material you will use. No time spent on preparation is wasted as it will always pay dividends in prolonging the life of the finished decorations, thus saving both time and money. No doubt you will all know some tips of your own, but hopefully this general guide will provide the simplest way to deal with large quantities.

WILD FLOWERS AND FOLIAGE

The following are all suitable for picking, and may be found growing wild:

Acer	Sycamore, in flower and fruit with leaves removed
Fagus sylvatica	Common beech
Heracleum sphondylium	Hogweed, cow parsnip
Malus	Crab apple, in flower and fruit
Petasites hybridus	Butterbur, leaves
Prunus spinosa	Blackthorn, in flower
Quercus	Oak, in flower
Reseda lutea	Wild mignonette
Reseda luteola	Dyer's rocket, Weld Rose hips
Smyrnium olusatrum	Alexanders
Sorbus aria	Common whitebeam
Tilia	Lime, in flower
Verbascum thapsus	Mullein

When picking the above do please remember the following points:

1. It is illegal to uproot any wild plant.

2. Some wild plants are further protected by law making picking illegal.
In Norfolk the plants under this category are usually hard to find, grow in water or are too small for flower arranging. Do check what is available in your own area.

3. Some plants are rare, and should not be picked although it may not be an offence to do so. Amongst these are sea holly, spiked speedwell, milk parsley, all orchids, herb Paris, marsh fern and crested buckler fern.

4. Only cut materal from hedges and road verges.

5. If you only find one plant of a particular species, do not cut it.

6. Cut only what you are sure you really need.

7. Always cut carefully using secateurs. Pretend it is a prized plant in your own garden.

8. Only cut material you can identify.

9. Be careful about conditioning. A lot of wild material wilts so badly in a hot car or even a hot hand that it ends up on the compost heap.

10. Boil the stems of all woody material.

11. Carry a moist polythene bag or bucket of water with you.

12. *Umbellifers* (hogweed, Alexanders and cow parsley) are very useful but should only be picked when some fruit is developing, otherwise wilting will occur.

Appendix I

Finance and Ordering

The Dean and Chapter make an annual contribution to the Flower Guild, and although the amount does not allow for the purchase of many flowers, it does provide enough to obtain the oasis required, as well as other essential items. However, we rely on the generosity of the Guild members to produce most of the flowers needed each week. A small sum is available for anyone who needs a little help to buy a few extra blooms, and several flower clubs, without access to much home grown material, have accepted a contribution towards their costs enabling them to tackle larger projects involving more of their members.

When planning large events, we do take care to order direct from the nurserymen to benefit from the more reasonable wholesale prices. The extra effort in organising the order is well worth the time and trouble involved. This applies particularly to the the Easter flowers because they are certainly our largest single purchase of the year, and it is the only time when we ask our congregation for donations. Their generosity makes a tremendous difference, because not only do we then have enough flowers to decorate well, but our budget does not suffer too great a shock.

By far the bulk of the material, not only the greenery but the flowers for all the major events, is provided by the committee members. When weddings, funerals and memorial services are being prepared, the relatives normally contribute towards the costs, depending on their choice. The organisers of concerts and other special events usually donate the flowers, especially if they wish to have something extra.

We are fortunate in having some shrubs near the cathedral which were planted for Guild members to cut whatever they require, but we tend to leave these for emergencies, rather than depending on them for our weekly supply. There are also other trees in the Close whose foliage is most useful at different seasons. We are especially grateful to people who let us pick or cut from their gardens, because as anyone who has offered well knows it is no good expecting us to take half a dozen two foot pieces when we need readily available quantities.

If all our known sources of generosity have been used, we then have to fall back on florists' flowers, which we always do for weddings and similar events. I am including a simple guide to ordering, but don't forget that these decorations are on a very large scale, and you might receive an unpleasant shock if you order in such quantities without considering where the flowers are to be placed.

This guide, for flowers only, has been based on the order placed for the BMA event in July, which is described in the chapter on Summer flowers.

The large pedestal arrangements prepared in the green tubs needed on average: 50 flowers made up as follows:

10 Delphiniums,	tall	4-6ft (1.25-2m)
20 Lilies	medium	3-4ft (0.9-1.25m)
20 Gladioli	medium	as above

| 10 Spray carnations | short | 1 ½-2 ½ft (45-70cm) |
| 10 Mixed blooms | short | as above |

The above, plus a lot of mixed foliage, should provide plenty of variety.

On the same basis, when planning a pedestal arrangement of more normal proportions, you should allow for:
30 tall blooms:

7 Delphiniums
13 Gladioli
10 Lilies
10 Spray carnations
10 Assorted short stemmed flowers

A small low decoration on a tomb will require a mixture of about 30 short stemmed blooms.

There is one other important point to remember when using this guide; the size as well as the number of blooms must be considered. Take, for example, the difference between dahlias, freesias and sweet peas which will effect the quantity required. Dahlias are inclined to have very brittle stems, so some loss should be taken into account when ordering. The stems and blooms of the smaller freesias vary considerably; they are usually used when some scent is required and when they can be viewed at close quarters. Sweet peas do not go very far, so make sure plenty are ordered. These examples are in marked contrast to the more substantial flowers. If the blooms are in tight bud they will appear rather thin, but once they have had time to develop they will rapidly fill out.

The quantity required can also be effected by the choice of colour, as paler shades require a greater number of flowers. If a particular colour is needed to match something, a bridesmaid's dress for example, it is wiser to select a deeper shade because when flowers are mixed together they lose their depth of colour, and a lot of foliage will drain the effect. When the lighting is inadequate bright shades are needed in order to be seen. I think you will be surprised how even the brightest can be toned down when they are in a mixed arrangement. These points are particularly worth considering when ordering bridal flowers. In order to save money it is always sensible to try different alternatives by substituting a seasonal flower for one that has to be specially ordered – it is often possible to save pounds.

These should be sufficient guidelines to enable anyone to order flowers for any occasion with confidence.

Appendix II

Tools of the Trade

everal items are absolutely essential if large scale decorations are to be attempted. They fall into two categories, cathedral equipment kept in the flower store and personal tools. I have a shopping basket which has been adapted to carry everything I might possibly need. It has been lined with some strong cloth, and stitched to provide a series of pockets. The bottom has a removable plastic sheet which can easily be cleaned. It usually contains the following:

Bin liners, plastic
Candleholders for placing in floral foam
Floral foam tape
Floral ribbons, as required
Garden twine, green
    Three ply plain jute fillis
Gloves, rubber kitchen type
    Strong gardening pair for prickly plants
Gutter tape
Loppers, pair long handled 22in (56cm)
Pliers
Scissors, florist's
Secateurs, lightweight
    Heavy duty
Stay Soft flower base
Weights, rarely needed in the cathedral
Wire, florist's, various gauges
Wire-cutters

Needless to say a lot of additional, so called useful, items find their way into the basket, but it has saved a tricky situation more than once. The contents may sound excessive, and a smaller basket would certainly hold most people's needs. If every eventuality is catered for the work can be undertaken quickly, because so much time is saved by having everything to hand. The bin liners are most useful for carrying flowers and foliage, and a great help in keeping different types of material separate. When filled they can be packed easily standing up or on their sides in a car, and where small flowers must be placed upright or are still in their pots, the watertight quality of the liners is a tremendous help.

CATHEDRAL PROPERTY

Cleaning Materials   Sweeping brushes
                         Hand brushes
                         Dustpans
                         Floor cloths
                         Buckets

Containers	From copper urns to plastic bowls, tubs and troughs of all sizes, washing-up bowls and even jam jars
Donkey cloths	Five foot square cloths with handles for carrying material
Floral Foam	There are several products available, but 'Oasis' is the brand known to most arrangers. The bricks absorb enough water to increase their weight from 2oz (56gm) to almost 4lb (1.8k), taking up nearly 3pts (1.5l) after about two hours. If they are allowed to dry out completely they will not easily reabsorb moisture, but they can be reconstituted by plunging them in very hot water or by pouring boiling water over them. If used oasis is not required for some time it can be kept moist by storing it in a plastic bag, and will be reusable after many weeks, even months.
	Foam can be purchased in both brick form and small round blocks ideal for table centres. It is also obtainable in made-up rings of different sizes, but these are only suitable for short periods. There are also blocks made specially for dried flowers.
Flower Buckets	Tall buckets with two handles
Flower Cones	Various sizes, some with points
Garden Canes	To support the flower cones
Oasis	See **Floral Foam**
Pedestals	Wooden pedestals of various sizes and adjustable wrought iron ones
Step-Ladders	Strong wooden step-ladders which must be stable for arranging, and light aluminium steps preferably with platforms for watering.
Trolley	Low loading trolley
Wire Netting	Chicken wire of various gauges from 0.5in to 1.5in, but mostly the latter. A supply of wire, originally used as rabbit netting around young forestry plantations, was removed once the trees became established, and is reused for decorating, a considerable saving as netting is quite expensive.
Miscellaneous	Hanging baskets, artificial flowers for Christmas.

Regrettably security must be considered even in a cathedral, because it is surprising how many things disappear, and I would suggest that all equipment, whether cathedral property or personal, should be clearly marked. Some time ago a man, who had broken into our shed, was seen leaving the cathedral by a gate at the north-east corner with three of our step-ladders under his arm. Fortunately the steps were well marked, and luckily he walked straight into the police at the gate. Two of our members were not so fortunate, and had their handbags stolen at Easter, one from within the cathedral and the other from her car. The items we most frequently have to replace are washing-up bowls, watering cans, buckets, brooms and secateurs. I am sure that in the majority of cases they are only borrowed, but we rarely see them again. Occasionally if everyone is told that such and such an object has gone missing, it does return. We always warn Guild members to be very careful when they leave their handbags or keys. The problem has increased over the last few years, and no doubt is not unique to East Anglia, but it is sad nevertheless. Finally, to end this short chapter, the roster lists should always be pinned up where they can be seen easily. At Norwich the arrangements are as follows:

High Altar	– Two pedestals
Nave	– Two large arrangements in wall brackets
West Door	– One pedestal
Jesus Chapel	– One small pedestal
Bauchon Chapel	– One small pedestal

The rest are prepared by the committee, and any extra displays required at the south door or crossing are decorated with the surviving blooms from the previous week.

Glossary

A short list of ecclesiastical terms which the decorator may encounter. The majority are common to most places of worship, but several refer specifically to Norwich Cathedral.

Altar	Holy table, usually at the east end, but also in other positions, or placed in an area reserved as a sanctuary. Flowers are now seldom placed on the altar in this country.
Altar Rails	Rails enclosing the Sanctuary which should not be decorated.
Ambulatory	Covered walk in the cloisters or the cathedral, usually a semi circular or polygonal aisle enclosing an apse.
Apse	Semi circular or polygonal recess, usually with an arched or domed roof.
Boss	Knob or projection, often carved, normally at the intersection of the ribs in a vault.
Chancel	Area east of the crossing in a cathedral, as far as the High Altar rails.
Chapter	See **Dean and Chapter.**
Clerestory	Upper storey of nave walls in a cathedral or large church, pierced by windows.
Cloisters	Usually an enclosed quadrangle, walled on the outside, with a covered colonnade.
Colours, Liturgical	Heraldic colours which are clear, strong and harmonious are used throughout the Church year, according to the season: 　　red – scarlet 　　green – bright green 　　blue – Prussian blue 　　gold – golden yellow 　　silver – use white The following colours are used at the different seasons, according to the festivals: 　　Advent – blue or violet 　　Christmas – white 　　Epiphany – white and green 　　Lent – violet 　　Easter – white 　　Pentecost – red

Trinity – green

Crossing   The point where the transepts meet.

Dean and Chapter   The cathedral's personnel include the following:

Dean – Responsible for the overall management of the cathedral and staff.

Canon Treasurer – Responsible for finance and in charge of the Close.

Canon Precentor – In charge of music and the choir.

Canon Vice-Dean – Custodian of the fabric, and responsible for the upkeep of the building.

The three Canons, who together form the Chapter, work on a three monthly rota as Canons in Residence, providing the priestly presence with overall responsibility for the spiritual and pastoral care in the cathedral.

Cathedral Officials:

Organist and Choir Master

Sacrist – Responsible for the daily running of the cathedral furniture and services.

Vergers – Part of the Sacrist's department.

Visitors' Officer

Fair Linen   Linen altar covering for services.

Font   Receptacle for baptismal water. (Flowers should not be placed on the top or within the bowl without special permission.)

Honorary Canons   Retired priests who help with the cathedral services.

Lectern   Book stand on which the Holy Bible is placed for reading aloud.

Liturgy   The words of the main offices (services) of the day, Mattins, Evensong and Holy Communion.

Misericords   Shelves, often carved, underneath the choir seats which tip, and were used by the monks to lean on.

Muniments Room   Room off the Triforium at the east end of Norwich Cathedral used for storage.

Nave   The main body of the building west of the crossing or chancel.

Paschal Candle   Large candle on a tall free standing candlestick lit during services from Holy Saturday to Ascension Day.

Presbytery   Part of the church or cathedral at the east end, reserved for the officiating priests.

Reredos   Ornamental carved or painted wood screen behind

	and above the altar, occasionally made of stone.
Sacristy	Room generally set aside for vestments and sacred vessels.
Screen	In Norwich Cathedral it divides the nave from the east end and choir stalls.
Transepts	Parts of the building at right angles to the nave, thus forming a cross-shaped church.
Triforium	The middle storey of a church, treated as a gallery or arcade, above an aisle or over the arches of the nave and choir, also known as the Tribune gallery.
Vestry	Room attached to a church or cathedral in which vestments are kept, and where the clergy robe.

Bibliography

Baillie, The Revd. John L.: *Meditation in Flowers*, Clarius Publications, Dorset, 1967.

Banks, Roger: *Living in a Wild Garden*, World's Work Ltd., Surrey, 1966.

Bean, W.J.: *Trees and Shrubs, Hardy in the British Isles*, John Murray Ltd., London, 8th edition, four volumes and supplement, 1970.

Berrisford, Judith: *The Wild Garden*, Faber & Faber Ltd., London, 1966.

Best, Margaret: *Growing and Arranging Church Flowers*, A.R.Mowbray & Co. Ltd., Oxford, 1982.

Boland, Maureen and Bridget: *Old Wives' Lore for Gardeners*, Bodley Head Ltd., London, 1976.

Bridges, Derek: *Flower Arranger's Bible*, Century Hutchinson Ltd., London, 1985.

Chatto, Beth: *The Dry Garden*, J.M.Dent & Sons Ltd., London, 1978.

Coutts, J, Edwards, A, Osborn, A and Preston, G.H.: *The Complete Book of Gardening*, Ward Lock Ltd., London, 1954.

Culpeper, Nicholas: *Complete Herbal*, 1st published, London, 1653, reprinted by Omega Books Ltd., Hertfordshire, 1985.

Davies, Jennifer: *The Victorian Kitchen Garden*, BBC Books, London, 1987.

Duff, Gail: *A Book of Pot-Pourri*, Orbis, London, 1985.

Emberton, Sybil: *Growing Plants for Flower Arrangement*, Wisley Handbook 20, RHS, London, 1975.

Encyclopaedia Britannica, 1973 edition.

Fox, Robin Lane: *Better Gardening*, R & L, Oxfordshire, 1982.

Greenaway, Kate and Marsh, Jean: *The Illuminated Language of Flowers*, Macdonald and Jane's Publishers Ltd., London, 1978.

Hay, R. and Synge, P.M.: *The Complete Dictionary of Garden Plants*, Ebury Press and Michael Joseph Ltd., London, 1969.

Hay, R., McQuown, F.R. and Beckett G. and K., *The Dictionary of Indoor Plants in Colour*, Ebury Press and Michael Joseph Ltd., London, 1974.

Hay, R., Edited by, *Reader's Digest Encyclopaedia of Garden Plants and Flowers*, Reader's Digest Association Ltd., London, 1971.

Hellyer, A.G.L.: *Shrubs in Colour*, W.H.& L.Collingridge Ltd., Middlesex, 1966.

Hillier and Sons: *Hillier's Manual of Trees & Shrubs*, Winchester.

Hynson, Sandra S,: *Homage Through Flowers*, Washington Cathedral, DC, 1978.

Kaye, Reginald: *Ferns*, Wisley Handbook 32, RHS, London, 1978.

Jekyll, Gertrude: *Colour Schemes for the Flower Garden*, Country Life Ltd., 8th edition, London, 1936.

Johns, The Revd. C.A.: *Flowers of the Field*, George Routledge & Sons Ltd., London, 1853.

Lloyd's: *Encyclopaedic Dictionary*, Edward Lloyd Ltd., 1895.

Macqueen, Sheila: *Church Flower Arranging*, Ward Lock Ltd., London, 1982.

Pearce, Erica Lady: *The Permissive Garden*, Sweethaws Press, Sussex, 1987.

Perry, Frances and Greenwood, Leslie: *Flowers of the Wild*, Hamlyn Publishing, 1972.

Petch, Dr.C.P. and Swann, E.L.: *Flora of Norfolk*, Jarrold & Sons Ltd., Norwich, 1968.

Preston, F.G.: *The Greenhouse*, Ward Lock & Co. Ltd., London, 1951.

Purefoy, Molly: *Arranging Church Flowers*, C.Arthur Pearson Ltd., London, 1964.

Robinson, William: *The English Flower Garden*, John Murray, London, 1883.

Robinson, William: *The Wild Garden*, 1st published by John Murray, London, 1870, reprinted by Century Hutchinson Ltd and The National Trust, London, 1983.

Spry, Constance: *Favourite Flowers*, J.M.Dent & Sons Ltd., London, 1959.

Spry, Constance: *Flower Decoration*, J.M.Dent & Sons Ltd., London, 1934.

Spry, Constance: *Flowers in House and Garden*, J.M.Dent & Sons Ltd., London, 1937.

Spry, Constance: *Garden Notebook*, J.M.Dent & Sons Ltd., London, 1940.

Squire, David: *Which Plant?*, Deans International Publishing for W.H.Smith, London, 1985.

Step, Edward: *Wayside and Woodland Trees*, Frederick Warne & Co. Ltd., London, revised 1940 edition.

Taylor, Jean: *Flowers in Church*, A.R.Mowbray & Co.Ltd., Oxford, 1976.

Vaughan, Mary Jane: *The Complete Book of Cut Flower Care*, Christopher Helm, London, 1988.

Wyman, Donald: *Wyman's Gardening Encyclopaedia*, MacMillan Publishing Co., New York, 1977.

Journals

Flora, The Magazine for Flower Arrangers and Florists.
The Garden, The Journal of the Royal Horticultural Society.
The Field.

Index

Abies procera 111
Absinth 109
Acanthus spinosus 93, 108, 116
Acer negundo 109, 110
Acer platanoides 109
Achillea filipendulina 'Gold Plate' 114
Achillea ptarmica 'The Pearl' 112
Aconitum 113, 115
Adiantum, Maidenhair 20, 106, 111
Advent ring 69, 78, 107
Agapanthus africanus 112, 115
Alchemilla mollis 38, 45, 47, 49, 113
Alstromerias 20, 38, 45, 48, 113, 115
Althaea rosea 48
Amaranthus 113, 114
Aminoid compound 102
Ananas comosus 'Variegatus' 95
Angelica 100, 113
Anthriscus cerefolium 38
Apple blossom 28, 100
Arborvitae 111
Archangelica officinalis 102
Artemesia absinthium 109
Artichoke 93, 109
Artificial flowers 78, 82
leaves 78
Arum lilies 17, 18, 19, 112
Asparagus officinalis 38
Asparagus plumosus 111
Aspidistra 110
Asplenium 95, 106, 111
Aster novi-belgii 113
Atriplex halimus 108
Atriplex hortensis 'Rubra' 108, 109
Aucuba japonica 95, 107, 110
Azalea 28

Baby's breath 44, 45, 46
Balsam 100
Barberry 30, 109
Bath tub 38
Baubles 69, 72
Bear's breeches 93, 108, 116
Beech 49, 58, 117
Beehive 46, 64
Bells of Ireland 103, 113
Berberis vulgaris 109
Bergenia leaves 110
Berries 106
Bird cherry 93
Bird's nest fern 95
Black-eyed Susan 113
Blossoms 25, 114
Blue 11, 33, 99, 123
Blue gum 44
Boiling water treatment 116, 117
Borage 100
Borago officinalis 103
Box 18, 45
Broom 20, 27, 100
Broom handle 47
Bucket 15, 31
Buxus sempervirens 18, 45, 78

Callistephus chinensis 114
Campanula medium 115
Campanula persicifolia 38
Campanula pyramidalis 54, 115
Candle 69, 88
Candle, Paschal 18, 20
Candlesticks 63
Canterbury bell 113
Cardoon 105, 106, 108, 115
Carnations, spray 20, 44, 46, 119
Ceanothus impressus 88
Cedar 100, 111
Chamaecyparis obtusa 'Crippsii' 63
Chamaecyparis pisifera 47, 111
Chimney flower 54, 115
China aster 114
Chincherinchee 44
Choisya ternata 95
Christ's thorn 102
Christmas 75
Chrysanthemums 58, 64, 67, 82, 100, 113, 114, 115
Chrysanthemum, white daisy 20
Chrysanthemum frutescens 'Marguerite' 45
Chrysanthemum maximum 112
Cinereria maritima 44, 110
Clematis montana 112, 115
Cloisters 35, 123
Colours, liturgical 123
Columbine 100
Conditioning 116, 117
Cornus 109
Corylus maxima 109
Cotinus coggyria 109
Cotoneaster 44, 63, 67, 106
Coumarin 102
Cross, straw, 63
Crown Imperial 102, 113
Cryptomeria japonica 45, 49, 78
Cupressus sempervirens 18
x *Cupressocyparis leylandii* 58, 64, 78, 87, 111
Cupressus macrocarpa 'Donard Gold' 88
Cutting 116, 117
Cynara cardunculus 108, 115
Cytisus scoparius 20, 26, 88, 95, 113

Daffodils 17, 20, 22, 93, 100, 112, 113
Dahlias 44, 49, 58, 100, 113, 114, 119
Daucus carota 47
Delphinium 38, 112, 115, 118, 119
Dianthus 112, 114, 115
Digitalis 101, 106, 112, 116
Dogwood 107
Donkey cloths 26
Dracaena reflexa 'Variegata' 95
Dried Flowers 93
Dryopteris 106, 111
Dutch iris 115

Echinops ritro 'Veitch's Blue' 38

Elaeagnus ebbingei 'Gilt edge' 107, 109
Elaeagnus pungens 'Maculata' 38, 95, 103, 107, 110
Eremurus robustus 113
Ethylene gas 7
Eucalyptus 44, 45, 109
Eucomis punctata 113
Euonymus 106, 107, 110
Euphorbia 18, 107, 113, 114, 116
Euphorbia pulcherrima 78, 80, 82, 87, 103, 114

Fagus sylvatica 26, 27, 38, 49, 63, 67, 117
Fagus sylvatica 'Riversii' 33, 63, 109
False castor oil plant 95, 110
Fatheaded Lizzie 95, 110
x *Fatshedera lizei* 95, 110
Fatsia japonica 95, 108, 110
Fennel 39, 101
Finance 118
Foeniculum vulgare 39
Forsythia x intermedia 17, 18, 113
Foxgloves 101, 106, 116
Freesias 20, 44, 45, 116, 119, 120
Fritillaria imperialis 102, 113
Fruit 63, 100
Fuchsia, hardy 63

Garlands 100
Garrya elliptica 107, 109
Gerbera 116
Gladioli 31, 33, 45, 58, 101, 112, 113, 114, 118
Gladioli, butterfly 46
Glass tanks 35
Glastonbury thorn 102
Gold 99, 110
Golden elder 44
Golden rod 101, 110, 114
Grapevine 101
Green 99
Grey 99
Guernsey lily 115
Gypsophila paniculata 44, 45, 46

Hanging baskets 47, 48, 76, 78
Harvest festival 63
Hawthorn (*Crataegus*) 30, 102
Hedera 22, 30, 38, 64, 69, 80, 82, 84, 93, 107, 110,
Helichrysum splendidum 44
Helleborus occidentalis 27
Hemerocallis citrina 'Baronii' 38
Holly 69, 80, 82, 93, 100
Hollyhocks 48
Hosta 44, 110, 112
Hydrangea 93, 115
Hydrangea paniculata 112
Hypericum calycinum 47, 113

Ilex 84, 93, 100
Ilex x altaclarensis 80, 84, 93, 103, 110

127

Ilex aquifolium 69, 78, 80, 82, 84, 87, 88, 103, 109
Iris hybrids 112, 113, 115, 116
Ivy 22, 69, 80, 83, 84, 93, 100

Japanese cedar 45
Japanese holly fern 111
Jekyll, Gertrude 7, 126
Juniperus communis 111

Kniphofia 113, 114

Ladder fern 93
Lady's mantle 38, 45
Larch (larix) 26, 111
Larkspur 33, 115
Lathyrus odoratus 112, 115
Laurel 60, 100, 101
Laurel, Portugal 38, 111
Laurus nobilis 101, 107, 110
Laurustinus 95
Lavatera trimestris 112
Leyland cypress 58, 64, 72, 78
Ligustrum ovalifolium 'Aureum' 18, 20, 49, 105, 108
Ligustrum vulgari 18
Lilac 100, 112, 115
Lilies 64, 67, 100
Lilies, Arum 17, 18, 112
Lilium candidum 102, 112
Lilium longiflorum 18, 112
Lily of the valley 99
Lime (tilia) 45, 106, 111
Loosestrife 38
Lotus flowers 99
Love-lies-bleeding 114
Lupinus arboreus 113
Lupinus polyphyllus 112, 113, 115
Lysimachia punctata 38

Madeira ivy 110
Magnolia 25
Magnolia grandiflora 93
Mahonia bealei 88
Mahonia x 'Charity' 95, 111
Mahonia japonica 18
Mahonia lomarifolia 108
Mallow 103
Malus pumila 26, 27, 114, 117
Maple, copper 33
Matthiola incana 112, 115, 116
Michaelmas daisy 100, 113
Molucella laevis 63, 103, 110, 113
Monkshood 33, 115
Montagu, Lady Mary Wortley 100
Myrobalan 58, 109

NAFAS 11, 40
Narcissus 112, 113
Nephrolepis exaltata 93

Nerine sarniensis 115
Nicotiana affinis 112
Noble fir 111
Norway spruce 72, 78, 84

Oak (quercus) 100, 105, 111, 117
Oasis 14
Onobrychis viciifolia 103
Ornithogalum thyrsoides 44
Osmunda regalis 111

Paeonia officinalis 112, 114
Paliurus spina-christi 102
Paschal Candle 20, 124
Passiflora middletoniana 103
Pews 44, 45
Peruvian lily 38, 40, 114
Phlox 112, 114
Phormium colensoi 108
Phormium tenax 95, 109
Picea abies 78, 84, 111
Picea glauca 72
Pineapple 95
Pineapple lily 113
Plaintain lily 30, 44, 110
Poinsettias 80, 87, 103, 114
Polystichum 111
Pot-et-Fleur 91, 100, 107, 111
Primroses 22
Privet 49, 100
Prunus avium 27, 112, 114
Prunus cerasifera 58, 109
Prunus 'Kanzan' 26, 27
Prunus laurocerasus 106, 111
Prunus lusitanica 38, 107, 111
Prunus padus 93
Pyrethrum roseum 114
Pyrus salicifolia 109

Red 33, 99
Red hot poker 113, 114
Rheum palmatum 'Atrosanguineum' 108
Rhododendron 27
Rhododendron ponticum 95
Ribbon 47, 78, 82
Ring mould 20, 63
Robinson, William 8, 28, 30, 126
Rocket 44
Rodgersia tabularis 108
Rosa allium 102
Rosa gallica 102
Rosa rubrifolia 109
Roses 31, 49, 93, 100, 112, 114, 115
Rose of Sharon 47, 101
Rose petals 101
Rosemary 101
Rudbeckia hirta 113

Saint-foin 103

Salix caprea 20
Salvia sclarea 'Turkestanica' 38
Sambucus racemosa 'Plumosa Aurea' 38, 44, 110
Sawara cypress 111
Scabious 33, 116
Sea ragwort 44, 45, 63, 110
Senecio leucostachys 105
Senecio maritima 44, 45, 63
Senecio Przewalskii 44
Shasta daisy 112
Shell flower 103, 110, 113
Silver 109, 123
Smoketree 109
Snowball bush 111
Solidago x hybrida 93, 114
Solomon's seal 111
Sorbus aria 25, 117
Spleenwort 106, 111
Spindle 110
Spinning gum 109
Spotted laurel 110
Spruce 72, 78
Spry, Constance 8, 126
Spurge 113, 114
Stephanandra incisa 20, 111
Stock 44, 101, 112, 116
Sweet pea 112, 114, 115, 119, 120
Sword lily 112, 113, 114, 115
Syringa vulgaris 112, 115

Tasmanium blue gum 109
Taxus baccata 78, 93, 111
Thuja plicata 'Aureovariegata' 58, 63, 106, 111
Transpiration 35
Transport 15
Troughs 44
Tulip 101, 112, 113
Tussie-mussie 101

Urns 11

Viburnum 95, 111
Violet 99, 123

Waterers 17, 59
Weigela florida 109, 115
Weigela praecox 'Variegata' 45, 110
Western red cedar 58, 63, 106
White 99, 123
Whitebeam 25, 105
White spruce 72
Wild flowers 117

Yellow 99, 123
Yew, English 78, 93, 95, 111

Zantedeschia aethiopica 17, 18, 19, 112